Ready, Set, Move!: A 30-Day Faith Journey for Kids
Published by Parent Cue, a division of The reThink Group, Inc.
5870 Charlotte Lane, Suite 300
Cumming, GA 30040 U.S.A.

Interested in buying devotionals for the kids in your church or community? Get discounted rates on quantities of 10 or more at parentcuestore.org or orangestore.org.

ISBN: 978-1-63570-198-2

©2023 Parent Cue

Author: Jon Williams and Brandon O'Dell

Lead Editor: Lauren Terrell
Creative Direction: Ashley Shugart
Project Manager: Brian Sharp
Director of Parent Cue: Hannah Joiner Crosby
Director of Publishing: Mike Jeffries
Design & Layout: Sharon van Rossum
Illustrations: Studio Muti
Framework: 252 Kids Team

Printed in the United States of America
First Edition 2023

1 2 3 4 5 6 7 8 9 10

03/08/23

A 30-DAY FAITH JOURNEY FOR KIDS

BY JON WILLIAMS & BRANDON O'DELL

CREATORS OF THE SO&SO show

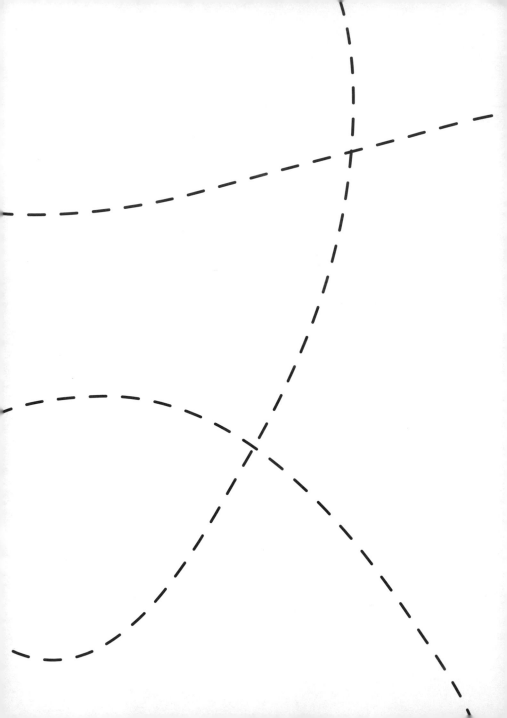

INTRODUCTION

Hello everyone! I'm Jon.

And I'm Brandon!

And you're reading *Ready, Set, Move! A 30-Day Faith Journey for Kids.*

That's a big title. Our readers will probably have questions.

Then . . .

WHAT IS A DEVOTIONAL?

A devotional is a book you **devote** time to that helps you learn or grow in some way.

THERE'S MORE ➞

HOW MUCH TIME DO I HAVE TO DEVOTE?

The book is designed to be read in 30 days. But here's the thing. It doesn't have to be 30 days in a row. You could spread it out over a few months if you want. Read at your own pace. You could even finish sooner than 30 days if you're a speed reader.

WHY IS IT CALLED "READY, SET, MOVE"?

This book is all about faith. And more specifically, faith in Jesus. What is faith? What does it mean to have faith? Is faith just believing or is there more to it? The writer of Hebrews refers to faith as a "journey." With any journey, you have to get ready and set . . . to move!

WHAT EXACTLY IS THE SO & SO SHOW?

I'm so glad you asked. *The So & So Show* is a show where we learn about the Bible and how to live and love like Jesus. You may have seen the show at your church, on the internet, or on an app called Parent Cue.

And if you haven't seen *The So & So Show* before, use the camera on a smartphone to check it out!

Brandon and I are the hosts of *The So & So Show*.

AND we're the writers of this book.

So pack your metaphorical bags, come on board, and join us on a journey of discovering more about God, Jesus, and this thing we call faith.

Ready! Set! MOVE!

7

KEY

When you see this handsome mug, it means that Jon is talking.

This is your signal that Brandon is talking.

A compass points you in the right direction. When you see this, it means you're about to read from the Bible.

This is when our friend, Kellen, is making an excellent point.

This shows up when you're getting instructions for what to do next.

This will pop up whenever we **REVEAL THE QUESTION!**

Use a smart phone camera whenever you see a QR code to get bonus content from *The So & So Show*.

DAY ONE, HERE WE COME!

A JOURNEY OF FAITH

HEBREWS 12:2A

Have you ever been on a journey? Maybe you didn't call it a journey. Maybe you called it a trip. Or a voyage. Or a vacation. Have you ever started off someplace and then traveled for a while and ended up someplace different? If you have, then you've been on a journey.

There are different kinds of journeys, of course. You could journey from home to school. You could journey hundreds of miles to your favorite amusement park. You could journey over the river and through the woods to grandmother's house.

No matter where you're journeying, it's usually a good idea to prepare. Check the weather. Map out your path. Pack all of the necessities.

So let's prepare! Imagine you're about to go on a journey for a few days. You'll need to pack a suitcase. Question for you:

WHAT WOULD YOU PACK?

Jon, what is your ideal packing list when you're going on a trip?

Oh. That's easy, Brandon. Chocolate covered raisins.

. . . That's all?

Fruit. Dairy. That covers the two food groups.

So much wrong with that. Don't you think you should pack some essentials? A good book? A change of clothes? A toothbrush?

Oh, yeah! A toothbrush! I'll need that after all those raisins I eat.

That's what I thought.

In the suitcase below, write or draw the items you'd like to take with you. Use the provided list of words or write your own words. No right or wrong answers here. This is just an imaginary journey.

Toothbrush

Ice Cream Sundae

Television

Underwear

iPad

Trail Mix

Toothpaste

Book

Milkshake

Fish

Hairbrush

Crayons

Phone Charger

Sleeping Bag

Deodorant

Trampoline

Pencils

Microwave

Paper

Socks

Dog

Shirts

Shorts

Cat

Great! You're packed and ready to GO. That's really the point, isn't it? To GO somewhere. That's what a journey is. So let's GO somewhere. Let's GO on the most important journey of your life. A journey of faith.

 "Let us keep looking to Jesus. He is the one who started this journey of faith. And he is the one who completes the journey of faith."
Hebrews 12:2a NIrV

Here's one definition of the word faith:

Faith: Trusting in what you can't see because of what you can see.

You might not be able to see God, but you can see the things God has created. You can see how God has helped people in the past. And you can see how God moves in your life and the lives of people around you today. You can trust God is there even though you can't see God. That's faith.

Now if that doesn't come easy to you, that's okay. The writer of Hebrews said that you are on a "journey of faith."

And we know that some journeys take time. Your faith journey will last your entire life!

So how can you prepare for this journey of faith? You don't need a suitcase. You don't need to check the weather. All you need is right there in that verse on page 13. You just need to "keep looking to Jesus."

By reading about Jesus in the Bible, you can learn the best way to love and the best way to live. Ask God to prepare your heart and your mind for what you need to learn about faith.

Okay, we think you're ready to GO. **Every journey begins with a first step.** And you'll learn more about what that first step is on Day TWO.

THE FIRST STEP

JOHN 3:16

When you journey out of the country, you need something called a passport. It's a little book with your picture in it and a bunch of pages in the back to keep track of all the places you've been. So here's a question for you . . .

WHERE HAVE YOU BEEN?

 Inside the passport on page 17, draw pictures of all the different journeys you've been on. Or design a logo for the places. Or just write descriptions of your trips.

If you haven't been on enough journeys to fill the boxes, fill them up with journeys you'd like to take OR leave them blank and come back once you've been someplace new.

Brandon, where was your favorite trip ever?

That's easy, Jon. I spent a week in Hawaii once. It was amazing! There was a green sand beach, a black sand beach, an active volcano, beautiful sunsets! I'd love to go back someday. What about you?

This one time I saw the Eiffel Tower, the Sydney Opera House, and Machu Picchu, on the same day.

Aren't those places all on different continents?

Oh, for sure. My favorite trip is to the travel agency. You wouldn't believe how many brochures they have!

That's quite a trip!

Every journey begins with a first step. You can plan all you want. You can pack everything perfectly. You can map out every detail, research every rest stop, and plan every inch of the trip. But without that first step, you haven't really gone anywhere. It's the same with faith.

Remember our verse from yesterday? The writer of Hebrews said that Jesus "started this journey of faith." Jesus is the beginning. Looking to Him is the first step. So let's take a quick look at Jesus' journey.

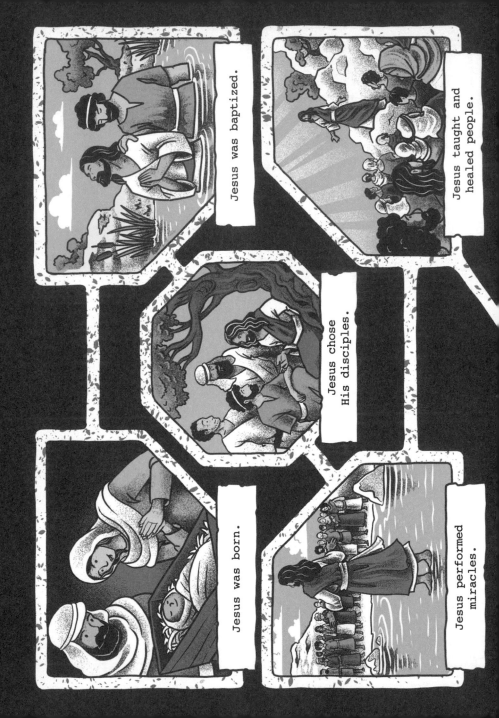

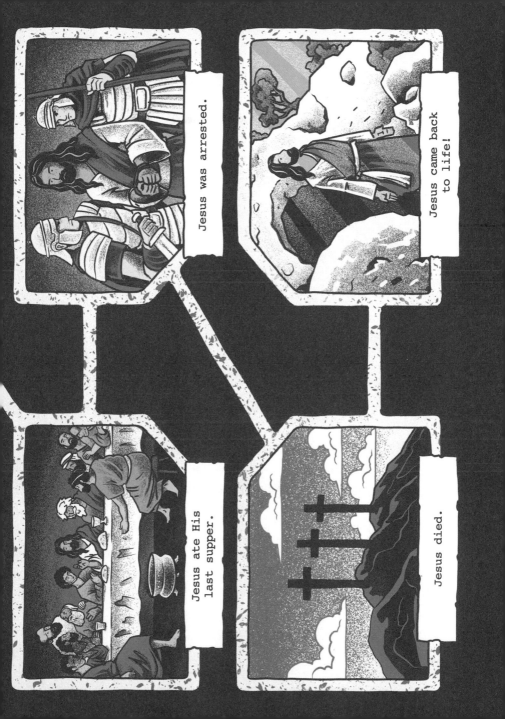

Wow! What an amazing journey! Jesus was born, lived a life of loving people, and He showed God's power. Then, even though He'd done nothing to deserve it, He was arrested and sentenced to die. He died to pay for the sins of the world! You would think that death would be the end of His journey, but no! Jesus came back to life in three days, proving God is even more powerful than sin and death!

AND HERE'S THE GOOD NEWS!

Jesus made it possible for you to have a relationship with God that will last forever!

 "God so loved the world that he gave his one and only Son. Anyone who believes in him will not die but will have eternal life."
John 3:16

If you look really closely at that verse, you'll see what the first step is on a journey of faith. To have faith, you don't have to memorize the Bible. You don't have to go your whole life without messing up. You don't have to be perfect. **The first step on a journey of faith is to . . . BELIEVE.**

If you're not sure what you believe right now, that's okay. Talk to someone you trust about what you're thinking and feeling. Or ask God to show you the best way.

If you have made the choice to believe in Jesus—either today or some time before—talk to God about what's next now that you've taken that first step. Where do you go from here?

On Day THREE, we'll learn about a man who was just starting out on his journey of faith. See you then!

PAUL'S TRAVEL DIARY— THE ROAD

ACTS 9:1-9

One person you'll learn a lot about if you read the Bible is a guy named Paul. Paul planted churches all over the place and wrote letters that would make up a good chunk of what we call the New Testament.

But even someone like Paul had a first step on his journey of faith. If Paul had kept a travel diary, it might have looked something like this:

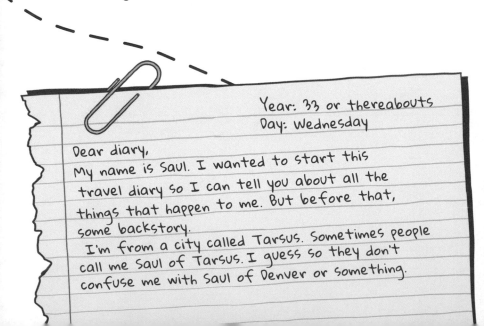

Year: 33 or thereabouts
Day: Wednesday

Dear diary,
My name is Saul. I wanted to start this travel diary so I can tell you about all the things that happen to me. But before that, some backstory.
I'm from a city called Tarsus. Sometimes people call me Saul of Tarsus. I guess so they don't confuse me with Saul of Denver or something.

FUN FACT TIME WITH KELLEN

Hey, everyone. I'm Kellen. Sorry to interrupt. You'll usually see me telling the Bible Story on *The So & So Show.* But today, I'm here with a fun fact about Paul. Or, uh, Saul. Saul actually had two names. Saul was the name he was born with, his Jewish name. And Paul was his Greek name—the name he went by to help him relate to people from other nations. So whenever you're reading the New Testament and you read about a guy named Saul or a guy named Paul . . . same guy. Hey, just for fun, try changing one letter in your name to make a new one. Write it here:

I think I'd change my name to Jellen. Or Tellen. As in, I'm going to keep Tellen you some fun facts later in this book.
Ha ha ha! LOL! See you soon!

tents. But here's the most important thing
used to you need to know about me.
be It is my mission to have all Christians
was
thrown in jail. I am on my way to the city of
Damascus to make that happen. My future is
looking so bright!
So much brighter than I thought.

ME IN TARSUS

Day: Sunday

Dear Diary,

I can hardly believe the last three days! I was on the road to Damascus because I was hoping to arrest some followers of Jesus there. But something happened. On the journey, I saw a light from heaven shining all around me! It was so bright I fell to the ground! And then I heard a voice say,

"'Saul! Saul! Why are you opposing me?'" (Acts 9:4)

I asked who it was, and the voice said, "'I am Jesus . . . I am the one you are opposing.'" (Acts 9:5)

After that, I opened my eyes, and I couldn't see anything! I had to be helped into the city. But even though I couldn't see, I felt like my eyes were open for the first time! I thought Jesus was a criminal. I thought that when He died on the cross, He stayed dead. But if He can appear to me in a light on a road, He's way more powerful than I thought. This turns my whole world upside down! I can't wait to tell you more later!

Paul's journey of faith began in a really remarkable way. I'm guessing your first encounter with Jesus wasn't in a blinding, bright light. But it doesn't mean your journey of faith is less dramatic. **When you know Jesus, it changes the way you see everything.** It can turn your world upside down.

As you continue to learn more about the things Jesus said and did, you'll start to see the world differently. Jesus can help you love others more deeply. He can help you worry less about things that aren't important. He can help you serve, trust, and forgive. When you pray, ask God to open your eyes. There may be things that God wants you to see that you haven't seen yet. Ideas you've never thought of. Bible verses you've never quite understood. With help, you can learn to see things the way God sees them.

On Day FOUR, your journey continues. Jesus has a clue to where you're headed.

SAND AND ROCK

MATTHEW 7:24-29

Whoa. What is happening? The book is upside down. This is a whole different way of reading. If you haven't already, flip the book over. I wouldn't want you to hurt your neck.

That's better. Now, if you get confused about what to read next, follow the instructions so you'll know what direction you're headed.

Directions are important on a journey. Especially if you feel like your world is upside down. Sometimes we use a map for directions. Sometimes we use GPS. And sometimes we rely on other people to give us directions. Let's see how good you are at giving directions.

REVEAL THE QUESTION

HOW DO YOU GET FROM YOUR BEDROOM TO YOUR KITCHEN?

THIS WAY!

In the space below, write out directions for someone who's never been to your home describing how to get from your bedroom to your kitchen. Be specific. What turns are there? How many doors will they pass? How many steps will it take? Any pets to watch out for? Will there be ice cream at the end? Go.

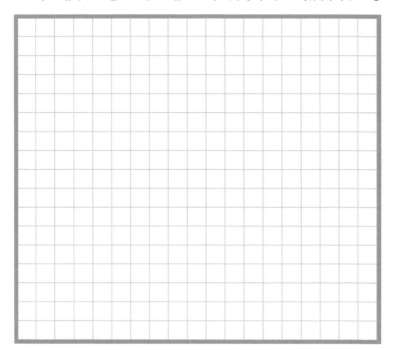

Great job! It's so helpful to have directions. Especially when you aren't sure where you are. (Now turn that page.)

Directions are also helpful on your journey of faith. During His
years on earth, Jesus spent a lot of time teaching people the
best way to live. The words He spoke can be like directions
for your journey. Here's just one of the things Jesus taught:

"'So then, everyone who hears my words and
puts them into practice is like a wise man. He
builds his house on the rock. The rain comes
down. The water rises. The winds blow and beat
against that house. But it does not fall. It is built
on the rock.'" **Matthew 7:24-25**

So a person who hears what Jesus says and then does what
Jesus says is wise. It's like they've built their house on a rock.
Then Jesus talked about another kind of person.

"'But everyone who hears my words and does not
put them into practice is like a foolish man. He
builds his house on sand. The rain comes down.
The water rises. The winds blow and beat against
that house. And it falls with a loud crash.'"
Matthew 7:26-27

The first kind of person hears what Jesus says and then does
what Jesus says. That person is wise. Their house is prepared
for the storm. The second kind of person hears what Jesus

says and then doesn't do what Jesus says. That person? Not so wise. Their house won't survive the storm.

Notice that both kinds of people HEAR what Jesus says. The difference is that one DOES what Jesus says, and one doesn't.

It's so important to read your Bible so you can know what Jesus taught. He said so many things that can help you on your journey. But knowing what Jesus says is only part of it.

Brandon, do you remember that time we tested which was stronger, sand or rock?

I remember it like it was yesterday.

It was yesterday.

Then my memory is correct.

Check it out here!

If you want to be wise, you have to DO what Jesus says. That way you'll be prepared for any storms along your way.

Here's your direction—DO what Jesus says. In the first four books of the New Testament, we can read about what Jesus said, did, and told us to do. On Day FIVE, you'll learn about the most important thing Jesus said to DO.

FLIP OVER

THE GREATEST COMMANDMENT

MATTHEW 22:34-40

Whew! You're right side up again. The instructions should have helped you not get lost. It's always nice to have a guide. Maybe you could be a guide for Kellen!

 Kellen has gotten lost on his way to *The So & So Show*. On the next page, help him get through the maze to Jon's basement studio. Then comeback here. If you need a hint, the solution is printed on page 194.

Well done! You helped Kellen complete his journey! You're an excellent guide!

On this journey of faith you're taking, you have a guide too! Your guide is, of course, Jesus. The first step on your journey is to BELIEVE in Jesus. That's very important! But there's more to it. If you want to be wise, you need to do more than just BELIEVE in Jesus, you also have to DO what Jesus says. And what did Jesus say? Let's find out.

In the first book of the New Testament, a man named Matthew wrote down a lot of what Jesus taught. One day

Have you ever gotten lost, Jon?

Do cats have 32 ear muscles?

I don't know.

Can fleas jump 350 times their own body length?

I've never measured.

Is Barbie's full name Barbara Millicent Roberts?

How could I possibly know that?

Yes. Yes, I've gotten lost. What about you? Have you ever been lost?

Yes. Now.

when Jesus was teaching, some really smart people called Pharisees came to question Him. They asked Jesus, out of all God's commandments, which one was the greatest.

They were talking about the commandments you can find in what we now call the Old Testament. Back then, the Pharisees called the rules from God "the Law." You've probably heard of **The Ten Commandments**. Things like—

DO NOT MURDER.
DO NOT STEAL.
HONOR YOUR FATHER AND MOTHER.

There are actually hundreds of commandments that you may not know. Like—

Do not cut the hair on the sides of your head.
Leave the crops in the corners of your field for the poor.
Stand up to show respect for old people.

The Pharisees asked Jesus to pick the greatest of all those commandments. Here's what Jesus said:

"Jesus replied, 'Love the Lord your God with all your heart and with all your soul. Love him with all your mind. This is the first and most important commandment.'"
Matthew 22:37–38

Everyone would have been very satisfied with this answer. LOVE GOD. Of course, that's the most important commandment. That's the greatest thing we can DO. But Jesus wasn't finished . . .

> "'And the second is like it. Love your neighbor as you love yourself. Everything that is written in the Law and the Prophets is based on these two commandments.'"
> Matthew 22:39-40

Jesus said that loving your neighbor was one of the greatest things you can DO. And your neighbor isn't just the person who lives near you. A neighbor can be anyone and everyone. So . . .

The greatest commandment = **LOVE God. LOVE others.**

Think about some ways you can show LOVE to God. Write one thing you could do here.

_____

_____

_____

_____

Now think of a way you can LOVE others. Write it here.

_____

_____

_____

_____

Of course, there are lots of different ways to show LOVE. And coming soon, you'll learn more about what that looks like in your life. But first, on Day SIX, a *So & So Road Show!*

DAY SIX

Hey, everybody. So, we thought it would be fun if Jon, Brandon, and I went on a road trip around the country . . . and let you be a fly on the wall! Well, not really a fly. You're human, of course. But, by writing scripts of our journey at least you get to listen in on our conversations. So, enjoy reading the adventures we had on the road!

THE SO & SO ROAD SHOW—EPISODE 1
(HEBREWS 11:1)

As we look out over flat land, we see an empty road, when . . . far off in the distance . . . appears a tiny yellow car sputtering along.

Oh, and it has a sunroof.

And who exactly is riding in this tiny little car in the middle of nowhere? Jon is at the wheel driving, Brandon is in the passenger seat, and Kellen is scrunched up in the backseat.

BRANDON
Hey, everybody! I'm Brandon!

                    JON
    And I'm Jon.

                    KELLEN
    And I'm cramped . . . I mean, Kellen!

                    JON
    And we are just about to cross over
    the state line of Colorado to see-

                    BRANDON
    -the ROCKY MOUNTAINS!

                    KELLEN
    And breathe in all that fresh
    mountain air!

                    JON
    And pet a goat!

Kellen and Brandon look at Jon.

                    JON
    I'm just sayin' . . . there are goats
    in mountains.

Kellen decides to change the subject.

                    KELLEN
    Let's see how close we are to
    the mountains.

                    BRANDON
    Good idea!

*Brandon brings out a paper map. Kellen
is shocked.*

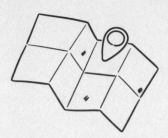

            KELLEN
What is that?

           BRANDON
A map.

            KELLEN
Ah. So, no GPS?
No cellphone directions?

           BRANDON
What? No! Those things are
unreliable. I just like the good ol'
fashioned paper map. And according
to my calculations, we should
be entering the Rocky Mountain
Staaaaaaate . . . NOW!

            KELLEN
MOUNTAINS!

            JON
MOUNTAINS!

*However, instead of mountains they see . . .
nothing but flat land. They stare out in
silence with big goofy grins until-*

Suddenly-

           BRANDON
WHERE ARE THE MOUNTAINS!!?

            JON
WHERE ARE THE MOUNTAINS!!?

Brandon buries himself in the map as Jon gets worried.

> BRANDON
>
> Wait, is this map wrong?

> KELLEN
>
> Uh, fellas . . .

> JON
>
> Are we LOST!?

> KELLEN
>
> Guys?

> BRANDON
>
> Maybe we're in the wrong Colorado!

> KELLEN
>
> Hey, guys!

> JON
>
> WHY is there more than ONE Colorado?!
> WHO WOULD DO THAT!?

> KELLEN
>
> HEY FELLAS!!

> JON
>
> How are we gonna eat!?

Brandon begins eating the map.
Yes. EATING THE MAP!

WELCOME TO

COLORADO

BRANDON

All we have for food is this map!!

KELLEN

GUYS!!

Brandon stops eating the map. Jon snaps to attention.

KELLEN

SORRY. Look, everything is fine. I'm almost positive the mountains haven't gone anywhere.

BRANDON

Well, my eyes say differently.

KELLEN

All I'm saying is . . . have a little faith, fellas. Just 'cause you can't see something doesn't mean it isn't there.

In fact, maybe this is a good time to think about something other than "MISSING MOUNTAINS". Mind if I share a verse?

KELLEN

Check this verse out:

"Faith is being sure of what we hope for. It is being sure of what we do not see."
Hebrews 11:1

KELLEN

So, we came here looking for
mountains, but we don't see
mountains, right?

JON

Right.

BRANDON

Right.

KELLEN

And we all know mountains don't just
get up and move on their own, right?

JON

Right.

BRANDON

Right.

KELLEN

But Brandon has a map that says the
mountains are there.

BRANDON

That's true. They're still on the map.

KELLEN

And I've been to Colorado before so
I know I've seen the mountains once
already. And, Jon, you saw the road
sign that CLEARLY stated we were in
the right state.

                    JON
Unless there's another . . .

                    KELLEN
There's not another state
named Colorado.

                    JON
Okay.

                    KELLEN
So even though we don't see the
mountains right now, we can be sure
they're there, because of what we
have seen. It's the same with God. We
may not have seen God, but we can be
sure God is there, because we have
seen what God has done and what God
is doing . . .

                    JON
MOUNTAINS!

                    BRANDON
MOUNTAINS!

*Suddenly, the mountains start to come into
view. They look like they are growing right
out of the ground in front of them. They
are beautiful.*

Jon, Kellen, and Brandon are mesmerized.

                    JON
Whoa!

>
BRANDON
Whoa!

KELLEN
See fellas? Sometimes, it's best to
have faith.

BRANDON
It's so beautiful!

JON
I think I might cry.

KELLEN
Yeah. It is pretty spectacular.

They stare in wonder. In silence.

And then, Jon squints a little.

JON
AND . . . I think I see a goat.

PAUL'S TRAVEL DIARY – ANANIAS HELPED PAUL

ACTS 9:10-19

So, remember that guy Paul we mentioned a few days back? Wait . . . you might remember him as Saul. ANYWAY, the guy with TWO names?

Hey, Brandon. You know what a GOAT is?

Yeah. A little four-legged animal that looks like a dog with a beard and horns?

No. GOAT! G. O. A. T. Stands for "Greatest of All Time."

Oh, right, right. No. Never heard of it.

Okay. Well, I was just thinking. Like, what are the GOATs? Like, what is the greatest food of all time?

Easy. Tofu.

Uh huh. Yeah. Tofu's . . . good. BUT . . . I would have said pizza.

Huh. Weird. Hey, I have an idea, let's ask them!

Who?

The person reading this conversation right now.

YEAH! Great Idea.

Down below, there's a list with some blanks next to each item. Write out what you think is the greatest thing in each category. Like for "FOOD," you might—

Tofu.

Yeah. We . . . we heard you the first time.

REVEAL THE QUESTION

WHAT ARE YOUR GOATS?

Greatest food: _____

Greatest movie: _____

Greatest sport: _____

Greatest video game: _____

Greatest musical instrument: _____

Remember how he wasn't always the biggest fan of Jesus or His followers, but after a miraculous encounter with Jesus on the road to Damascus, he changed his tune a bit? If he had kept a travel diary, his next entry may have looked something like this:

Year: 33 or thereabouts
Day: Saturday

Dear Diary,
Umm . . . WOW! So three days ago, I encounter Jesus on the road to Damascus and BOOM. I can't see. Well, the guys who were with me took me into Damascus where I stayed with a guy named Judas. He lived on Straight Street, I think.

Anyway, things are a little intense, you know? So, I did the best thing I knew to do. I started praying. And, as I started praying, I saw this vision in my head. A man placing his hands on my eyes and BOOM. I could see again. And wouldn't you know it? That same day a man named Ananias came to visit me. I wonder if anyone else received a vision.

Ananias: How I See It

(A Memoir)

I received a vision today.

From God.

Yep.

God.

God told me to go to a house on Straight Street and place my hands on . . . Saul of Tarsus.

I have heard of this man.

The very thought of going near him terrifies me. I told God that I am a follower of Jesus.

I reminded God that Saul of Tarsus does NOT like followers of Jesus.

I told God he would, therefore, not like ME and possibly harm me.

I made this abundantly clear to God.

God told me to "Go!" anyway.

I was . . .

nervous. I wasn't sure how people would react to me now that I was a follower of Jesus. Especially after how badly I had treated them in the past.

Before I knew it, there was a knock at the door, and I was suddenly . . .

Afraid!!

Yep.

Afraid.

But I knocked on the door anyway.

Why?

Because God loves me.

I love God.

And if God can love me, then God can love Saul too. So I knocked. I walked inside, and I

heard a man's voice say, "'Brother Saul . . . you saw the Lord Jesus. He appeared to you on the road as you were coming here. He has sent me so that you will be able to see again. You will be filled with the Holy Spirit'" (Acts 9:17) And right away

It was gross, and amazing, everything all at once.

Something like scales fell off Saul's eyes and he regained his sight.

Just like God said he would.

So, of course, the next logical thing to do was baptize him.

So I did.

And then we ate. God is good. God is great.

God is so great. Ananias had every reason to be terrified of me, but out of his love for God, he came to see me and helped me see again. He listened to God.

God's love seems to have zero limits. If God can love me, and Jesus' followers can love me—once an enemy, now a brother—then God's love is for anyone and everyone. I think I'm gonna start telling more people about it. I'll let you know what happens next.
More later!

ME ON STRAIGHT STREET

Jesus said love was the greatest thing you can DO. Paul "saw" firsthand that God loves everyone. Even though he used to be an "enemy" of the people who followed Jesus, Jesus' love was given and shown to him anyway. And it changed Paul. Forever. Like Ananias, you should strive to **LOVE everyone— even your enemies.**

It may not be easy. It won't always be fun. And sometimes, you may think it's pointless. But as you continue to read the story God has written and discover how powerful the love of Jesus is, you'll see that God is on a mission to show the entire world what real love is—the kind of LOVE that can transform people.

So, what exactly does Jesus' love look like? Well, your journey continues on Day Eight. See you there!

WHAT IS LOVE?

1 CORINTHIANS 13

When some people go on a journey, they like to have something called an itinerary. It's a detailed list of all the places they want to visit, all the sights they want to see, and all the things they want to do. Some people schedule it down to the last minute so they don't miss anything on their journey. Now I want to ask you . . .

HOW WOULD YOU MAKE AN ITINERARY?

REVEAL THE QUESTION

On the next page, write out your itinerary for tomorrow. What's your plan? When will you get up? When do you have to be somewhere? How long will it take to do what you need/want to do?

Time	Activity

Come back tomorrow night, and answer this question:

Did you stick to your itinerary? _____

Jon, what's on your itinerary for today?

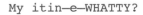

My itin—e—WHATTY?

Your itinerary?

My itin—e—WHO?

Your itinerary?

My itin—e—HUH?

YOUR ITINERARY! Haven't you read the other parts of this journal?

Not yet. Let me just put that on my schedule.

THAT'S YOUR ITINERARY!!

. . . My itin—e—WHEREY?

Never mind!

The apostle Paul went on a lot of journeys. When he became a follower of Jesus, he made it his mission to tell Jesus' story in as many places as possible. His itinerary may have looked something like this:

1. Go to Cyprus: Tell people about Jesus.

2. Go to Pamphylia: Tell people about Jesus.

3. Go to Phrygia: Tell people about Jesus.

4. Go to Lycaonia: Tell people about Jesus.

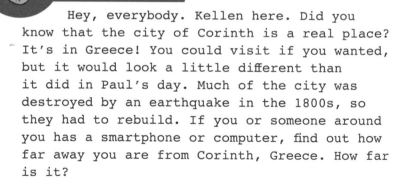

FUN FACT TIME WITH KELLEN

Hey, everybody. Kellen here. Did you know that the city of Corinth is a real place? It's in Greece! You could visit if you wanted, but it would look a little different than it did in Paul's day. Much of the city was destroyed by an earthquake in the 1800s, so they had to rebuild. If you or someone around you has a smartphone or computer, find out how far away you are from Corinth, Greece. How far is it?

It's over five thousand miles for me! Whoa. Maybe I'll see you there!

A lot of people followed Jesus because of what they heard from Paul. And a lot of churches were formed. Later, Paul would write letters to these churches to teach and encourage them. Many of those letters have become what we now know as the New Testament.

First Corinthians was a letter Paul wrote to a church in the city of Corinth.

In his letter to Corinth, Paul wrote about what LOVE looks like. An itinerary for LOVE.

"Love is patient. Love is kind. It does not want what belongs to others. It does not brag. It is not proud. It does not dishonor other people. It does not look out for its own interests. It does not easily become angry. It does not keep track of other people's wrongs. Love is not happy with evil. But it is full of joy when the truth is spoken. It always protects. It always trusts. It always hopes. It never gives up." Love never fails."
1 Corinthians 13:4-8a

In the verse to the left, circle the word LOVE every time it's mentioned. Next, look for the following things that describe love and underline them in the verse.

Patient

Isn't Proud

Never Fails

Doesn't Brag

Always Trusts

Always Hopes

Always Protects

Isn't Selfish

Kind

Not Easily Angry

As you can see, there are many ways to LOVE others. If you follow Paul's itinerary for LOVE, you'll not only be showing people how valuable they are, you'll also be doing what Jesus says is the greatest thing to DO.

Jesus Himself demonstrated LOVE in many ways. You'll see one of those ways on Day NINE!

JESUS WASHED THE DISCIPLES' FEET

JOHN 13:1-17

Have you ever been on a journey somewhere and looked up only to come face to face with . . . A FAMOUS PERSON? It can be pretty weird to see someone famous. You might just stare at them, frozen like a statue. You might forget how to talk. You might freak out and scream and end up acting like someone completely different . . . especially if it's someone who you really, really like.

But what if that person walked up to you out of the blue and said, "Hey! You wanna hang out?"

That would be insane—right!? Well, then, here's a question for you:

WHO IS SOMEONE FAMOUS YOU WOULD LOVE TO HANG OUT WITH?

Okay, there's a space down below where you can write the name of someone you'd love to hang out with. It could be a famous actor, musician, scientist, world leader . . . anyone!

If you have more than one person, make a list, you overachiever you, but it's not required. Then circle the one person who—if you met them—you might faint from excitement. Cool, now, remember that name, because we'll come back to it in a minute.

_____   _____

_____   _____

We don't know if they fainted from the excitement, but the disciples—those who followed Jesus—were definitely excited to hang out with Him. They learned so much from His teachings and through watching how He treated other people. Including them!

FUN FACT TIME WITH KELLEN

Hey, everybody. Kellen here. A little tidbit on the Passover Feast. It was a feast that was celebrated every year. Jewish people would take part in this feast as a reminder and celebration of when God set His people free from enslavement in Egypt. (If you haven't read that story, check it out in the first half of the book of Exodus!) It was a big deal.

Jesus and His disciples had gathered for a feast called Passover.

When gathering together, it was normal for a servant to wash people's feet. Yeah, I know it seems weird now, but back then people wore sandals or walked barefoot. And their feet would get really gross, all covered in mud and . . . other stuff that dropped out of animals . . . while walking down the road.

But when Jesus and His disciples gathered for Passover, Jesus did something totally unexpected. He got up from the table and . . .

"He poured water into a large bowl. Then he began to wash his disciples' feet. He dried them with the towel that was wrapped around him."
John 13:5

Jesus was being their servant. Yeah. The Messiah. The Teacher. The Son of God, Creator of everything . . . was washing His followers' filthy feet.

Peter, one of Jesus' followers, even tried to stop Jesus. His teacher and Lord shouldn't be washing his feet. It should be the other way around! Right!?

RIGHT!?

But Jesus insisted. He asked His disciples if they understood what He had done for them. And then He said:

"'You call me 'Teacher' and 'Lord.' You are right. That is what I am. I, your Lord and Teacher, have washed your feet. So you also should wash one another's feet. I have given you an example. You should do as I have done for you.'"
John 13:13-15

Remember that person you circled earlier? That person who might make you faint from excitement if you met them, let alone got to hang out with them?

Now, can you imagine them washing your feet? Better yet, would you even want them to? Ech. Chances are, they'd be too famous to stop and do something like that.

But Jesus, the One who didn't have to serve anyone at all but could demand to be served, God's perfect and holy Son . . .

. . . got down . . . and washed His own followers' feet. Like a servant. And then told them, and us too, that this is how we should treat each other. Talk about loving others! **You can love others by serving them.**

Look for simple ways to serve those around you today. (Maybe warn someone before you grab their feet and start washing them!) But Jesus didn't only teach us to love others. On Day TEN, we'll learn about a great way to show love to God.

JESUS CALMED A STORM

MARK 4:35-41

How do you feel about feet? Feet are great. They get you where you want to go on your journeys. They help you with your balance. But they can also be a little . . . gross. You know, some people have a fear of feet. And there's a name for it. It's called podophobia.

There are actually all kinds of fears that you'll encounter as you travel through life. (Hodophobia, by the way, is the fear of travel.) Which brings up the question . . .

WHAT ARE YOU AFRAID OF?

Write down the thing(s) you're afraid of in the space below.

There's probably a name for what you're afraid of. Something called a phobia. Here are a few:

➡ Fear of spiders: arachnophobia

➡ Fear of snakes: ophidiophobia

➡ Fear of heights: acrophobia

➡ Fear of speaking in public: glossophobia

➡ Fear of germs: mysophobia

➡ Fear of the dark: nyctophobia

FUN FACT TIME WITH KELLEN

There's a really unusual name for the fear of long words. And it's . . . before I tell you, if you have a fear of long words, you might want to look away because the fear of long words is called . . . hippopotomonstrosesquipedaliophobia!

So if you have that fear, you'd be afraid to say it out loud! The actual word for the fear is sesquipedalophobia. And then I guess someone thought it would be funny to add all those other letters, and it stuck. Not cool, dictionary people. Not cool.

If you want more fun with phobias, check this out:

Being afraid of things is perfectly normal. It means you're human. Jesus' disciples were afraid sometimes too, even when Jesus was with them.

There was one time, after Jesus had finished teaching a crowd of people, when He and His disciples got in a boat to cross over to the other side of the Sea of Galilee.

While they were traveling across the lake . . .

 "A wild storm came up. Waves crashed over the boat. It was about to sink. Jesus was in the back, sleeping on a cushion. The disciples woke him up. They said, 'Teacher! Don't you care if we drown?'" Mark 4:37-38

Pause. Sometimes just reading something doesn't give you the full effect of what it must have been like in real life. Imagine you're on a boat. And a storm comes up. The wind is whooshing all around you.

WHOOOOSH!!!

The waves are pounding against the boat.

SPLASH!!!!

There's so much water, THE BOAT IS STARTING TO SINK!!!

AAAAAHHHHH!!!

And Jesus, instead of helping, was SLEEPING IN THE BACK OF THE BOAT!!! You saw the terrified disciples wake Jesus up. They were probably screaming over the sound of the storm:

"'TEACHER!!! DON'T YOU CARE IF WE DROWN?????'"

Unpause. You won't believe what Jesus did next.

"He got up and ordered the wind to stop. He said to the waves, 'Quiet! Be still!' Then the wind died down. And it was completely calm.

"He said to his disciples, 'Why are you so afraid? Don't you have any faith at all yet?'"
Mark 4:39-40

So, in case you missed that . . .

JESUS TOLD A STORM TO STOP . . . AND IT DID!!!

He was asleep in the back of the boat because He wasn't afraid. He knew He could control the storm with a word.

This is how powerful God is. God is so much bigger than we are. God is so much bigger than anything we're afraid of. When we're worried or scared or terrified . . .

AAAAAHHHHH!!!

. . . God is still in control.

Jesus said the greatest thing you can DO is LOVE. LOVE God and LOVE others. So what's one way you can love God?

You can **LOVE God by trusting God.**

That means, when you're worried or afraid, remind yourself that God is more powerful than your fears. Trust God to take control whenever you experience a storm on your journey.

It doesn't mean you won't ever be afraid. You're still human after all.

Next time you're worried about or afraid of something, go to God with your fears. God is always with you. You'll learn more about that on Day ELEVEN.

DAY ELEVEN

GREAT COMMISSION/ ASCENSION

MATTHEW 28:16-20, ACTS 1:1-11

Jon, what are you afraid of?

Snakes, cockroaches, the ocean at night, tall trees, small trees, medium-sized trees, smelly cheese, being in tight spaces, being in wide open spaces, being in space, and the monster that lives in my closet. OH! And lists.

That's a lot.

What about you, tough guy?
What are you afraid of?

Not so much. I think the only thing
I'm really afraid of is being alone
. . . wait. Where did you go? Jon?
JON? JOOOOOOOON!!!!

What? I'm right here.

Oh. I thought you left.

I actually can't go anywhere.
I'm stuck to the page . . .
because this is a book.

Good point.

Some people like spending time by themselves. You might be by yourself right now, quietly reading this book. But there are times when people really don't like being alone. Like, for instance, if you're lost . . .

WHO WOULD YOU WANT WITH YOU IF YOU WERE LOST?

In the blanks below, write the name(s) of the people you would want with you in each situation. It could be someone you know, a family member or a friend. It could be someone well known. Or it could just be a type of person.

For example, if you were lost in a burning building, you'd probably want to be with a firefighter. No right or wrong answers here.

If I were lost . . .

in the woods, I'd want to be with _____.

in an airplane, I'd want to be with _____.

in the supermarket, I'd want to be with _____.

in the city, I'd want to be with _____.

underwater, I'd want to be with _____.

on a farm, I'd want to be with _____.

When Jesus died on a cross, His disciples must have felt alone. They were definitely afraid. But then . . .

JESUS. CAME BACK. TO LIFE!!!

After that, Jesus spent several days with His disciples, which reassured them that He was, in fact, alive. On one occasion, Jesus gathered all His disciples together and told them:

"'All authority in heaven and on earth has been given to me. So you must go and make disciples of all nations. Baptize them in the name of the Father and of the Son and of the Holy Spirit. Teach them to obey everything I have commanded you. And you can be sure that I am always with you, to the very end.'"
Matthew 28:18-20

Jesus gave His disciples a mission. To "GO and make disciples of all nations" (emphasis added). That's quite a task. ALL nations is a lot of nations. BUT Jesus also gave His disciples a promise:

"I am always with you, to the very end."

Jesus promised His disciples they would never be alone. He would always be with them. Later, Jesus explained a little more. He said:

> "'You will receive power when the Holy Spirit comes on you. Then you will tell people about me in Jerusalem, and in all Judea and Samaria. And you will even tell other people about me from one end of the earth to the other.'"
> Acts 1:8

Jesus wanted the disciples, just a few guys, to love others by telling EVERYONE His story. That was an impossible mission. Especially in a time without podcasts or even the postal service!

FUN FACT TIME WITH KELLEN

Have you ever thought about how many people there are in the world? At the time I'm writing this, there are close to 8 billion! That's 8,000,000,000 people. If you wanted to just say, "Hi" to every person individually, it would take you over 250 years. So, you'd better get started.

But don't forget Jesus' promise. "'I am always with you, to the very end.'"

Shortly after Jesus said all these things:

"He was taken up to heaven. The apostles [disciples] watched until a cloud hid him from their sight." Acts 1:9

Jesus was gone again. Did that mean He broke His promise? Nope. It just meant He would be with His disciples in a different way. Through the Holy Spirit.

And Jesus' promise wasn't just for the disciples. When you BELIEVE in Jesus and put your trust in Him, the Holy Spirit comes to live in you too! You are never alone.

Jesus' mission to tell EVERYONE about Him, to share His love with others, doesn't seem so impossible when you realize you won't be doing it alone.

The Holy Spirit will help you LOVE others. The Holy Spirit can give you words to say and can help you know the wise choices to make. For some people, the Holy Spirit is like a feeling they get. Some people hear the Holy Spirit like a gentle whisper inside.

When you pray, ask God to help you think of ways you can share Jesus' story with the world.

We'll learn more about how to SHARE God's love with the world as we continue our journey of faith. But first, on Day TWELVE, let's check in on *The So & So Road Show!*

DAY TWELVE

THE SO & SO ROAD SHOW-EPISODE 2
(PHILIPPIANS 4:8)

*Once again, we enjoy our three friends
Kellen, Jon, and Brandon as they travel.*

*Jon is in the backseat, Kellen is in the
passenger seat, and Brandon is driving.
Brandon is hunched over the wheel, sort of
like a vulture. He's not happy.*

>   JON
> Hey Brandon. You've been awfully
> quiet lately. You okay?

>   BRANDON
> *meh*

>   JON
> I'm sorry, I didn't catch that . . .

>   BRANDON
> *meh*

>   JON
> He says "meh", Kellen.

>   KELLEN
> Come on, Brandon. What's going on
> with you?

Brandon doesn't want to talk, but gives in . . .

> BRANDON
> Fine. If I have to.
>
> So. I've been really, really, REALLY looking forward to this trip because I wanted to show my two closest friends all of the amazing tourist attractions I've been reading about.
>
> BUT . . . so far NONE of them have turned out to be what I thought.

> KELLEN
> Whaddaya mean?

> BRANDON
> Well, for instance . . . the World's Largest Ball of Q-Tips was just a small ball of Q-Tips bunched together.

> JON
> It was tiny.

> BRANDON
> The self-proclaimed 'Most Exciting Flea Circus in the World' was just some fleas on a mangy dog.

> KELLEN
> A cute mangy dog, though.

BRANDON
The World's Tallest Roller Coaster
just turned out to be a giant coffee
table coaster that could roll . . .

KELLEN
It was a big coaster.

JON
Needed a big mug of coffee.

BRANDON
And THEN, the Hollywood Stars tour
turned out to be us looking at stars
in the night sky . . . in Hollywood!

JON
Okay. But, I'm still confused. You're
grumpy because . . . ?

BRANDON
BECAUSE I can't stop thinking about
how I've ruined our trip and wasted
my friends' time and money.

Jon and Kellen look at each other for a
second before . . .

KELLEN
ARE YOU KIDDING ME!!?

JON
ARE YOU KIDDING ME!!?

KELLEN
Brandon! We're having a great time!

                    JON
Yeah, man.

                  BRANDON
You're just saying that.

                    JON
Dude. You have to quit beating
yourself up. I thought everywhere you
took us was AWESOME!

                  BRANDON
Really . . . ?

                    JON
That giant COASTER was hysterical!

                   KELLEN
And that dog with the fleas really
was cute.

                  BRANDON
(sarcastic) Gee. Thanks.

                   KELLEN
Wait. I think I see what's going
on here.

                    JON
What?

                   KELLEN
All Brandon can think about is
everything he thinks has gone wrong!

JON
Dude, are you just thinking about all
the stuff that's gone wrong?

BRANDON
Maybe.

JON
That means "YES"! Kellen, you gotta
help him see the light!

KELLEN
Not a prob. This great Bible verse
just popped in my head. It's from
Philippians 4:8

"Finally, my brothers and sisters, always think about what is true. Think about what is noble, right, and pure. Think about what is lovely and worthy of respect. If anything is excellent or worthy of praise, think about those kinds of things."

JON
That's a cool verse.

KELLEN
It reminds us that spending our time
thinking about good things is great
for the soul.

JON
It also challenges us to find
something good or hopeful even in
otherwise difficult situations. And
this is possible when we remember the
hope we have in Jesus.

KELLEN
Thinking about the things God cares
about and values can bring more joy
to your day.

BRANDON
You mean things like spending time
with great friends? Laughing a lot?

JON
YEAH! That's what we're talkin'
about!

BRANDON
You're right! SO grateful for
you guys.

BRANDON
Hey, now that I'm in a better mood
. . . what say we go see the World's
Tiniest Piece of Rice!

And I promise that THIS time I won't
get mad if it's not super tiny.

JON
Either way, it'll be fun.

KELLEN
On to bigger and better things, or in
this case . . . tinier ones.

They all laugh as they drive down the road
to their next adventure.

YOU ARE THE LIGHT OF THE WORLD

MATTHEW 5:14-16

Ever had to ask for DIRECTIONS? Okay, okay. Calm down. It's just a question. Nobody else can hear you answer out loud. But, seriously, have you?

OF COURSE, YOU HAVE! Everyone has. Whether it's for a school assignment, putting a bike together, or driving somewhere, directions get us to our desired goal. Our destination. Hey, that brings up a great question . . .

REVEAL THE QUESTION

DO YOU KNOW ALL THE ROAD SIGNS DRIVERS USE?

Here's a quick test to see if you're paying attention when someone is driving around. Below are several road signs that drivers use to help them get to their destination safe and sound. Match the sign on the left by drawing a line to its meaning on the right.

Some are easy. Some are hard. But give it a shot.

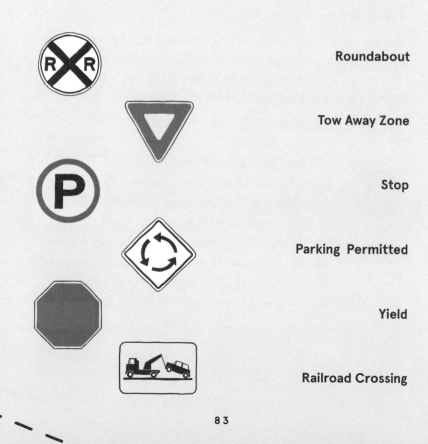

Roundabout

Tow Away Zone

Stop

Parking Permitted

Yield

Railroad Crossing

How'd you do? (You can check your answers on page 195.) Not bad? Not good? Well, good news is, if you're reading this devotional, you probably have some time to learn about ALL the signs before you start driving.

Now here's a really weird thought: If road signs help us get to our destination, what helps people get to God? I mean, have you ever seen a sign that says, "THIS WAY TO GOD!"

Well, the funny thing is . . . you probably have.

And Jesus told us about it.

See, one day Jesus was on a hillside speaking to His disciples and the crowd of people who were following Him around. And on this hillside, He gave an amazing lesson—a talk we often call "The Sermon on the Mount." During this sermon, Jesus said this:

"'You are the light of the world. A town built on a hill can't be hidden. Also, people do not light a lamp and put it under a bowl. Instead, they put it on its stand. Then it gives light to everyone in the house. In the same way, let your light shine so others can see it. Then they will see the good things you do. And they will bring glory to your Father who is in heaven.'" Matthew 5:14-16

Did you catch what the "road sign" pointing to God is?

Well, let's break this down a bit. When God's Holy Spirit lives inside of us, it acts as a guide. You might hear other people call a feeling from the Holy Spirit a "gut feeling" or "a tiny thought that pops in my head telling me right from wrong." The Holy Spirit definitely speaks to us that way. But, oh, it does so much more than that.

When we "listen" to the Holy Spirit and make choices that reflect who Jesus is, guess what happens?

We shine.

FUN FACT TIME WITH KELLEN

Hey, everybody. Kellen here with a fun fact that will blow your mind. Did you know that one of the brightest flashlights in the world can be seen almost an entire mile away!? Pretty impressive, right?

SO, have you guessed what "sign" points others to God?

It's you! When you decide to listen to the Holy Spirit and live your life in a way that reflects the way Jesus loves people, you become a sign pointing to Him. You become a light that shines on God by doing simple things like . . .

. . . helping someone with their homework.

. . . letting your sister or brother watch the show they want.

. . . being kind to friends at school who are having a bad day.

When you do things like this, you help others find their way to God. **We SHINE God's light by doing good things.**

You just have to be willing to let God's love SHINE through you.

Take some time and write down the names of people who have SHINED the love of Jesus into your life. And afterwards, maybe go thank them. Then, check out Day FOURTEEN for some ways YOU can shine.

_____

_____

_____

_____

_____

_____

PAUL'S TRAVEL DIARY— PAUL AND SILAS IN PRISON

ACTS 16:16-40

Light really makes a difference, doesn't it? You probably don't think about it a whole lot. But light plays a part in a lot of our journeys. For example . . .

REVEAL THE QUESTION

WHERE IS YOUR FAVORITE PLACE TO SEE . . .

a sunrise? _____

a sunset? _____

the stars? _____

Not only can light be beautiful to look at, but it can also be super helpful. Like when it's dark out, and you need to see where you're going!

Light made a big difference in Paul's life too, which is good, because in the next part of his travel diary, things get a little dark.

Year: A Long Time Ago
Day: Monday, Almost Tuesday

Dear Diary,

Well, we're in prison. Me and my buddy, Silas. And we didn't even do anything wrong! A few days ago, we were on our way to pray when this woman started following us. She kept shouting—

"These men serve the Most High God. They are telling you how to be saved." (Acts 14:17)

Now we had never met this woman, so how did she know that? Turns out she had an evil spirit inside her that helped her predict the future! And she followed us around FOR DAYS! All the time, shouting—

"These men serve the Most High God! They are telling you how to be saved!"

Finally, I just couldn't take it anymore. So I turned around and said,

"In the name of Jesus Christ . . . I command you to come out of her!" (Acts 16:18)

And then the evil spirit left her. Which you'd think was a good thing.

It turns out, though, that some people were using this woman to make money with her predictions. But since the evil spirit didn't live in her anymore, she wasn't able to make any predictions. No spirit, no predictions, no money. So Silas and I were stripped, whipped, and thrown in prison.

Now it's almost midnight and we're locked up in the dark with some other prisoners. They've even chained our feet so we can't run away. But where are we gonna go? It's not like we're gonna break through the prison doors!

Anyway, it's dark now, but there's still joy in our hearts because of Jesus. Gonna pray now.

Day: Tuesday

You've got to be kidding me! What a crazy day this has been!

Last night, after Silas and I prayed, we just started singing. Right there in the prison in front of all the other prisoners! We just started singing hymns to God. You know, singing about how amazing God is and how grateful we are.

And I'm sure the other prisoners were like: "You're in prison like the rest of us. What do you have to be so happy about?"

And then, while we were singing, the whole prison started to shake. It was an honest-to-goodness EARTHQUAKE! A real big one too. Every single prison door flew open. And

. . . AND! ALL THE CHAINS CAME LOOSE! We could've just walked right out the door. But we didn't.

The earthquake woke up the jailer, and when he saw all the doors open, he was sure we'd all escaped. I guess he couldn't see us in the dark. So he picked up his sword and was about to stab himself with it, when I shouted: "'Don't harm yourself! . . . We are all here!'"

He found a light and came in and saw us. And you could tell he was amazed. He knew this was more than just an earthquake. It was a miracle. He fell down on his knees and said: "'What must I do to be saved?'" (Acts 16:30)

And we said: "'Believe in the Lord Jesus. Then you and everyone living in your house will be saved.'" (Acts 16:31)

Then, in the middle of the night, the jailer took us to his house. He took care of us, fed us, and we told his whole household all about what Jesus had done for them. God is amazing. I'll never stop telling people!

Even on what could have been one of their darkest days, Paul and Silas chose to shine. They chose to sing and praise God. They chose joy. You can do that too! **You can SHINE God's light by choosing joy.**

Choosing joy is easy when everything is going your way. It's a little harder when your circumstances have gotten out of control. But even then, you can remind yourself that God loves you, God is with you, and God will make everything right in the end.

If you're having a bad time right now, ask God to help you see the light through the darkness. And make sure you talk about it with someone who loves you.

If everything's going great, ask God to help prepare you for those circumstances you can't control. Ask God to help you choose joy.

On Day FIFTEEN, you'll learn more ways to SHINE.

PETER WENT TO THE HOUSE OF CORNELIUS

ACTS 10

Have you ever been on a long drive with a bunch of people? Maybe you've ridden a bus to a weekend event with your church or gone on a faraway field trip with your school.

Things can get pretty boring. One way to pass the time is to have a sing-along, taking turns singing songs that contain words in a certain category. For instance, songs that have to do with the weather like:

"Singin' in the Rain"

"Let It Snow! Let It Snow! Let It Snow!"

"Somewhere Over the Rainbow"

"Umbrella"

"Here Comes the Rain Again"

Why don't you try?

WHAT ARE SOME SONGS ABOUT LIGHT?

Fill the car below with titles of songs that are about light, contain the word "light," or contain a word for the source of light (like sun, star, fireworks, etc.)

There's a car that's filled with light! You can try playing that game next time you're on a journey. Make sure to take turns with the people you're with. You want everyone to feel included.

One of Jesus' disciples, Peter, knew a little something about including people. But it was a lesson he had to learn . . . in a slightly unconventional way.

After Jesus had died, AND COME BACK TO LIFE, He put Peter in charge of leading the early church. Peter, along with the other disciples, was Jewish and back then, religious rules said Jewish people were not to associate with people who were not Jewish. If they did, it was possible that they'd become "unclean." (A person who was "unclean" couldn't hang out with their families or go to religious ceremonies. It was the ancient Jewish equivalent of having "cooties.")

This was a problem. You remember Jesus' mission to His followers to "go and make disciples of all nations"? It would be kind of hard to tell ALL nations about Jesus if you weren't allowed to hang out with some of them.

One day, around lunchtime, while Peter was praying on the roof, he had a vision from God!

Hang on. This story could use some sound effects. Try this:

If you don't have access to a smartphone, that's okay! You can provide your own effects. (Onomatopoeias are provided for your enjoyment.)

Peter was on the roof. And he was hungry. His belly started to growl.

 RUMBLE RUMBLE RUMBLE

Suddenly, he looked up and saw heaven open!

 KKKKKRAAAACKKK!!!

He saw something like a large sheet being let down by its corners.

 WHISH WHISH WHISH WHISH

The sheet had all kinds of four-footed animals on it along with reptiles and birds.

 NEIGH!!!! RUFF!! HISSS!!! OINK!!!

Then Peter heard a voice that said:

 "GET UP, PETER. KILL AND EAT" (ACTS 10:13).

Peter replied, "No, I won't! I've never eaten anything that isn't 'clean.'" And the voice said:

 "DO NOT SAY ANYTHING IS NOT PURE THAT GOD HAS MADE 'CLEAN'" (ACTS 10:15).

Three times this happened before the sheet was taken back into heaven.

 WHOOOSH!!!!!

When the vision ended, the Holy Spirit told Peter he should go with three men who had just shown up downstairs. Those three men were sent by a man named Cornelius who had been visited by an angel that told him to send for Peter. Only one problem here: Cornelius wasn't Jewish. And Peter had that whole religious rule thing to consider.

But the strange vision with the animals and the message from the Holy Spirit helped Peter see things in a new way. Maybe Peter COULD associate with people who weren't Jewish after all. So he invited the three men into the house as his guests. And the next day, Peter went with the three men to Cornelius' house.

When he went inside he said to them:

"'I now realize how true it is that God treats everyone the same . . . He accepts people from every nation. He accepts anyone who has respect for him and does what is right.'"
Acts 10:34-35

Then Peter told them the good news about Jesus. He carried out Jesus' mission by including people he thought had been left out. Everyone there who had heard Peter's message was filled with the Holy Spirit. And they were baptized.

You can be like Peter in your world. **You can SHINE God's light by including others.** Be on the lookout for people who aren't like you. Maybe it's people you haven't noticed before. Those people need to know how much God loves them, and you can help show them.

You're going to need help along the way, of course. You'll find out where that helps comes from on Day SIXTEEN.

VINE AND BRANCHES

JOHN 15:5-8

Brandon, you wouldn't believe the dream I had last night.

I bet I would.

I was in a cave searching for a treasure. There were cheese puffs everywhere. Like, when I'd step on the wrong rock, cheese puffs would come shooting out at me. Or when I tripped over a vine, cheese puffs would fall from the sky. But I got past them and then . . . I saw it.

The legendary golden cheese puff!

. . . I slowly picked it up and put it in my satchel. . .

But it was another trap! I started running! Cheese puffs were flying at me from all directions. Pew! Pew! Pew! I jumped over a huge hole in the ground, and I thought I'd made it, but then a gigantic cheese puff boulder started rolling after me. And when it was just about to smush me with cheese puff dust, I woke up. I have no idea why I dreamed that.

What'd you have to eat last night?

Cheese puffs. Why?

No reason.

One thing you'll need on every journey you take is fuel. Something that gives you power to keep going.

An airplane needs kerosene fuel.

A car needs gasoline or a battery.

A rowboat needs someone or something doing the rowing.

Even if your journey is on foot, you, a human being, need food and drink to provide you with energy. And the kind of fuel you put in your body will determine the kind of energy you have. Eating a bag of cheese puffs and a soda probably won't help you get to the top of a mountain. You need the right kind of fuel.

You'll need fuel on your journey of faith too. The right kind of fuel.

When Jesus and His disciples were sharing what would be their last supper together, Jesus said:

 "'I am the vine. You are the branches. If you remain joined to me, and I to you, you will bear a lot of fruit. You can't do anything without me.'"
John 15:5

If what Jesus said is confusing to you, that's okay. Jesus' own disciples didn't always understand the things He said. So let's look a little closer.

Jesus said that He was the vine.

Then Jesus said you are the branches. Now, He was talking to His disciples at the time, but let's imagine He was talking to you too. YOU are one of the branches.

 Draw a branch coming from the vine above. Your branch can wind anywhere you'd like on the page. Just make sure it's attached to the VINE.

If this were an actual grapevine, there would be lots of branches growing from the vine. But what would happen if the branches weren't connected to the vine? They'd stop growing!

It's the same with you and Jesus. When you aren't connected to Jesus, you won't grow spiritually. And like Jesus said, "You can't do anything without me."

But when you ARE connected, you grow. And not only that, Jesus said: "If you remain joined to me, and I to you, you will bear a lot of fruit."

 Go back to the branch that you drew and draw some fruit along your branch. Use different colors if you have them. Fruit is colorful!

Staying connected to Jesus is important. So what are some ways you can stay connected to Jesus?

One way is by reading the things Jesus said and did in the Bible. You're staying connected just by reading this devotional!

Another way to stay connected is by talking to God. You could make a habit of talking to God every day. At bedtime, when you wake up, when you eat a meal, or at 2:37 in the afternoon. God wants to hear from you.

You can also stay connected to Jesus by listening to His Spirit inside you—the Holy Spirit.

Can you think of another way to stay connected to Jesus?
Write it here:

_____

_____

_____

_____

When you're connected to Jesus, you'll bear fruit. Which is
good, because Jesus said,

"'When you bear a lot of fruit, it brings
glory to my Father. It shows that you are
my disciples.'"
John 15:8

You can SHINE by staying connected to Jesus. You can point
others to God just by staying fueled up, connected. Ask God
to help you stay connected to Jesus.

You definitely want to grow and bear fruit. And you'll find out
what kind of fruit on Day SEVENTEEN.

FRUIT OF THE SPIRIT

GALATIANS 5:22-23

Your packing list for a journey isn't complete until you've packed the most important thing—SNACKS! But for this journey, we're packing only healthy snacks.

FUN FACT TIME WITH KELLEN

Did you know that a cucumber is actually a fruit? It's true! It contains the seeds of a flowering plant, so by definition, it's a fruit. So are olives, zucchini, pumpkins, and peppers. And tomatoes too, but not everyone agrees. In 1893, the U.S. Supreme Court officially declared that a tomato was a vegetable. Now I'm confused what to put on my fruit salad . . .

In the word search on the next page, circle the names of fruits you can take with you on your trip. Beware the junk food! Don't circle those! If you find something that's junk food, draw a line through it.

Apple Plum Cantaloupe
Banana Kiwi Grape
Peach Watermelon Strawberry

```
J K E I F C A N T A L O U P E
E B A N A N A P I Z Z A Y Q J
I K U G U M M I B E A R S X Z
H A M W A T E R M E L O N T C
E I J J C A Z K I W I Z M G L
B U B B L E G U M Z P U H E I
S E L F C O N T R O L X J N C
J U C A N D Y F F P E G R T O
S V C H O C O L A T E O G L R
T A Z J C S O Z I R V O V E I
R O I E E Q G I T E M D I N C
A P C R U J R J H B U N D E E
W E E O Q L A X F T X E L S N
B A C A L J P R U J D S O S K
E C R T C H E L L O S P E N
R H E G X E N M N O X Y L A J
R P A T I E N C E V P P J S J
Y G M E C H E E S E P U F F S
D O U G H N U T S A K J T B T
P K I N D N E S S B M P I Z P
```

When you're on a journey of faith with Jesus, you're going to bear fruit. But not apples or bananas or strawberries.

The apostle Paul wrote a letter to a church in Galatia about what he called "the fruit of the Holy Spirit." He wrote:

 "The fruit the Holy Spirit produces is love, joy and peace. It is being patient, kind and good. It is being faithful and gentle and having control of oneself. There is no law against things of that kind." Galatians 5:22-23

When you see an apple tree, you expect it to have apples on it, don't you? When you see a peach tree, you expect it to have peaches. Well, if someone is a follower of Jesus, they have the Holy Spirit inside them, so you would expect them to have the fruit that Paul was writing about. Apple trees grow apples. Peach trees grow peaches. And God followers—God trees—grow God fruit!

Paul wasn't making a list of things for you to work on necessarily. It's more like the natural things that come from someone who stays connected to Jesus. God's fruit looks like love, joy, peace, patience, kindness, goodness, faithfulness, gentleness, and self-control. These are all attributes that God will grow in you as you stay close to Him!

So here's some more fruit for you to search for.

Go back to the word search from earlier and put boxes around attributes of the fruit of the Spirit. (The answer key is on page 196.)

Love, Joy, Peace, Patience, Kindness, Goodness, Faithfulness, Gentleness, Self-Control

Let's take a closer look at the list.

Love: You've learned this one already. Jesus said LOVE is the greatest thing you could DO. You can LOVE others by serving them. You can LOVE your enemies. And you can LOVE God by trusting God.

Joy: This is more than just being happy. It's reminding yourself that God loves you, God is with you, and God will make everything right in the end. You can choose joy even when things aren't going your way.

Peace: This can be similar to joy. It can be a feeling you get that everything's going to be okay. Peace can also be the ability to calm situations that may not be so peaceful.

Patience: No time for this one. MOVE ON!!

Kindness: When you're kind, you choose to think of other people before yourself. You give up your place in line. You let other people have their way.

Patience: Just kidding before. Of course there's time for patience. When you're patient, you're not easily upset when something is taking too long. You can be content while you wait.

Goodness: This isn't about being good at basketball or ballet. Being good is about doing good things. It can be about being generous with your time, talent, or energy.

Faithfulness: A person who is faithful is someone you can trust. If you give them a responsibility, they will not let you down. They're the kind of person you want in your life.

Gentleness: Some people think they're right all the time. And they want you to know it. When you're gentle, even if you ARE right, you have the attitude of someone who's willing to learn something new.

Self-Control: We usually learn what self-control is too late. AFTER we've eaten ALL that candy. Or AFTER we watched YouTube for SEVEN HOURS! Someone who controls themselves figures it out BEFORE it's too late.

This is the fruit that God grows in people who are connected to Him. Paul called this "living by the Spirit."

You'll see it in people around you. People who are **good**. People who are **patient** and **faithful**. People who always seem to **shine** with **joy**.

And guess what! **Others can see you SHINE when you live by the Spirit.**

Stay connected to Jesus, and people will be able to see God's fruit in you. Look at the different words above and talk to God about the ones you might need help with.

The fruit of the Spirit are things you can work on, sure, but mostly they're the result of you trusting God and staying connected to Jesus.

Coming soon on your journey, you'll learn a little bit about what you can TRUST God for. But first, on Day EIGHTEEN, let's check in on *The So & So Road Show!*

DAY EIGHTEEN

THE SO & SO ROAD SHOW-EPISODE 3
(ROMANS 12:16)

Once again, we join our friends Jon, Brandon, and Kellen on their cross-country adventures.

It's Jon's turn to drive. Kellen is resting in the back seat while Brandon enjoys a snack — a giant, RAW, ONION!!!

And Jon . . . "STRONGLY DISLIKES" onions.

The "crunching" Brandon makes while he eats is really grossing Jon out.

Jon rolls down his window slowly to let Brandon's onion breath leave, but it is not helping . . . AND JON CAN'T TAKE IT ANYMORE!

> JON
> BRANDON! You said the onion wouldn't smell!

> BRANDON
> Stop yelling. You're gonna wake up Kellen.

> JON
> Me!? The smell of that onion will wake him up before my yelling. Please. Just. Put it away.

Brandon thinks about it, then . . .

> BRANDON
>
> No.

> JON
>
> NO!?

Like a toddler, Brandon stares at Jon, and takes the biggest bite he can out of that onion . . . AND CHEWS WITH HIS MOUTH OPEN.

Jon brings the car to a screeching stop.

> JON
>
> That's it! OUT OF THE CAR!!

Jon and Brandon get out of the car and start yelling at each from either side.

> BRANDON
>
> You've done nothing but nag at me this entire trip. "Brandon, don't eat onions!", "Brandon, get your smelly feet off my dashboard!", "Brandon I can't see the road when you cover my eyes!"

> JON
>
> Well, this is my car! I'm paying for the gas! I'm trying to keep us safe on the road and you keep distracting me.

> BRANDON
>
> You smack your bubble gum.

                    JON
You sing the wrong words to every
song on the radio!

                  BRANDON
You scrape your teeth with
your fingernails!

                    JON
You smell like cheese!

                  BRANDON
I happen to like cheese!

                    JON
TOE CHEESE!?

                  BRANDON
Well, you . . . I can't think of
anything else so I'll just . . .
GRRRRRRR!

                    JON
GROBALARERR!

*Suddenly, a sleepy-eyed Kellen pops his
head out of the sunroof.*

                   KELLEN
Hey, fellas. What's up?

*Brandon and Jon just stare at each other
with angry eyes.*

                   KELLEN
Okay, looks like A LOT happened,

while I was asleep. Um, so, what's
going on here?

                    BRANDON
WELL, it all started when Jon yelled
at me for eating THIS onion!

                    JON
You told me the onion wouldn't smell!
AND IT DID!

                    KELLEN
FELLAS!!

Jon and Brandon stop.

                    KELLEN
I am sure there is a way we can work
this out. Unless you LITERALLY want
to split this car in half, we have to
ride together somehow.

Brandon and Jon look at each other.

                    BRANDON
Huh. You thinkin' what I'm thinkin'?

                    JON
I think I'm thinkin' what
you're thinkin'.

                    BRANDON
Then I think we should stop thinkin'
about what we're thinkin' and get to
what we're thinkin'.

JON
I think so.

MINUTES LATER.

Kellen is sitting in the backseat with a large piece of tape running from the top of his head all the way to the car's dashboard.

They "split" the car in half with a tape line.

KELLEN
This is not what I was thinkin'.

BRANDON
Glad you had the painter's tape, Jon. Otherwise we wouldn't have been able to divide this car in half.

JON
I'd say something back to you, but I can't hear you since you're on that side of the car.

BRANDON
Well, then, if you can't hear me, I guess you can't smell this onion either.

JON
You. Wouldn't. DARE!

Brandon bites the onion and blows his breath toward Jon.

JON

Can't . . . breathe.

KELLEN

Okay! I gotta be honest. You guys are acting like a couple of little kids. So, I'm just gonna drop some Bible knowledge on you two. Ready?

JON

K.

BRANDON

(mouth full)

Mmm-hm.

KELLEN

Read this and read it well, you two. It's verse 18 in chapter 12 of Romans.

"If possible, live in peace with everyone. Do that as much as you can."

Basically, it comes down to this. We have an amazing God who decided to make peace with us through Jesus. God could have totally decided NOT to do that . . . but instead, God chose to make peace with all of us. And as followers of God . . . well, we should do the same with each other. EVEN when we disagree.

So, Brandon? Is there anything you'd like to say?

BRANDON
Um . . . Jon. I'm sorry. I guess it was kind of rude of me to eat a smelly onion in a confined space when I know you strongly dislike onions.

JON
Well, I shouldn't have overreacted.

KELLEN
GREAT JOB! Proud of you two.

JON
Yeah. We were acting silly. Well, I guess we should get back on track and get a move on.

BRANDON
Jon. I'm still hungry. Do you mind if I finish my onion? You can roll down the window.

JON
Go ahead. IN FACT . . .

(Jon rips off half of the onion)

Give me some of that onion.

BRANDON
But you really, really dislike onions.

JON
Consider it an act of peace.

Jon takes a huge bite . . . and immediately realizes he's made a huge mistake. He tries to swallow it but instead coughs so hard it flies out of his mouth and all over the windshield.

BRANDON
Nice. Your "peace offering" is all over the windshield.

JON
I really tried to eat it . . .

KELLEN:
And with that, I'm gonna go back to sleep.

DO NOT WORRY

MATTHEW 6:25-34

Have you ever taken a journey on an airplane? Before the plane ever takes off, the flight attendants stand in front of the passengers and give a little presentation.

"When the seatbelt sign is lit, fasten your seatbelts. We recommend you keep your seatbelts fastened throughout the flight as we may experience turbulence."

Turbulence is when the air outside causes the plane to shift. It can make the plane feel like it's bouncing. Seatbelts sound reasonable.

"In the event of cabin decompression, oxygen masks will fall. Place it over your nose and mouth and breathe normally."

Um . . . Okay, so apparently there's a chance, probably not a very big one, that when you're on a plane, you'll run out of oxygen and have to breathe through a mask. Good to know.

"Should there be a water landing, your seat cushion can be used as a flotation device."

WHAT??? There's a chance the plane will have to land ON WATER??? What kind of presentation is this???

Okay, okay. Let's take a step back for a second. It's the twenty-first century. Flying on a plane is very safe. It would be EXTREMELY UNLIKELY for a plane to land on the water. So why the pre-flight warning? Here's what the flight attendants really mean—

"We've got this. We've been on thousands of flights like this. We are prepared for all the possibilities, even the EXTREMELY UNLIKELY ones. You don't have to worry."

Jesus made the same point around two thousand years ago. Not about flying in a plane, obviously. About journeying through life.

You probably remember learning about the Sermon on the Mount from earlier, when Jesus was teaching His disciples

I know you're not supposed to worry, but I still do sometimes. Check this out to see some of the things I worry about.

and the crowd that had gathered on a mountainside. Here's one of the things He taught:

"'I tell you, do not worry. Don't worry about your life and what you will eat or drink. And don't worry about your body and what you will wear. Isn't there more to life than eating? Aren't there more important things for the body than clothes?'" **Matthew 6:25**

Jesus was pretty clear right there, wasn't He? "Do not worry." We know we're supposed to not only hear what Jesus says but DO what Jesus says. And yet we still worry.

Let's try something.

There's a blank page right over here. You could also use a separate sheet of paper. Write down things that you worry about. It can be one thing or a list. If you're not worried about anything right now, you can skip this step.

So how do you keep from worrying when so many things are
. . . worrisome? Jesus went on:

"'Look at the birds of the air. They don't plant
or gather crops. They don't put away crops in
storerooms. But your Father who is in heaven
feeds them. Aren't you worth much more than
they are? Can you add even one hour to your
life by worrying?'" Matthew 6:26–27

Think about that! If God takes care of the birds, God will
surely take care of you, right? But there's more! Jesus
also said:

"'And why do you worry about clothes? See how
the wild flowers grow. They don't work or make
clothing. But here is what I tell you. Not even
Solomon in all his royal robes was dressed like
one of these flowers. If that is how God dresses
the wild grass, won't he dress you even better?'"
Matthew 6:28–30a

God takes care of the wildflowers too! You can trust God to
take care of you! Finally, Jesus said:

"'Put God's kingdom first. Do what he wants you to do. Then all those things will also be given to you. So don't worry about tomorrow. Tomorrow will worry about itself. Each day has enough trouble of its own.'" Matthew 6:33-34

You are going to worry about something at some point in your life. Because you're not perfect like Jesus was. But maybe hearing Jesus' words will help you worry a little bit less.

Tear the piece of paper from the book where you wrote your worries. Or pick up the separate sheet of paper. Now fold it into a paper airplane. If you need instructions, try this link:

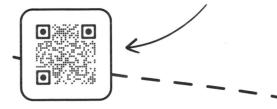

Once you've folded your airplane, launch it in the air, and let those worries fly away.

To sum up what Jesus said: God's got this. God knows what's happening and is prepared for all the possibilities—even the EXTREMELY UNLIKELY ones. You don't have to worry.

You can TRUST that God is in control.

If you're worried about something, talk to God about it. And talk to someone you love and who loves you. Talking your worries out is sometimes the best way to help them fly away.

 And remember that God is in control and has a plan. On Day TWENTY, you'll see God's plan in action. But not before things feel very out of control for Paul. So, fasten your seatbelts.

PAUL'S TRAVEL DIARY— THE SHIPWRECK

ACTS 27:1-28:10

Have you ever had to take a detour? Like, maybe you were on a journey and ran into a ROAD CLOSED sign. Or maybe you hit traffic, and you had to take a different route.

Or maybe you've been on a trip where things didn't work out the way you planned. Bad weather may have cancelled your day at the beach. Or the amusement park might have been shut down for repairs.

When things don't go the way you want or expect them to, it can be a real bummer. But it doesn't have to be.

Paul travelled the world telling people about Jesus. And a lot of the time, things didn't go how he planned. But he learned, time and time again, that his plan wasn't what was most important.

Year: The 60's AD
Day: I have no idea.

Dear Diary,

I'm on a boat. Still. Have been for who knows how long. Thought I'd write a little to pass the time. I was arrested a while ago for telling people about Jesus, and now we're sailing to Rome for my trial. It hasn't exactly been smooth sailing. But what can you do? We can only go where the wind blows us. At our last stop, I told everyone,

"Our trip is going to be dangerous. The ship and everything in it will be lost." (Acts 27:10)

But they didn't listen to me. So here we are, back on the water, still a long way from Rome. I'm going to wrap up for now. The wind is starting to pick up.

Day: Still no clue

I have to write fast! We're in the middle of a huge storm! It's been like this for days. The ship can't take much more! The crew has been throwing supplies overboard to try and lighten the load, but I know it won't help. Even so, I'm not afraid.

An angel came to me last night and said, "Do not be afraid, Paul. You must go on trial in front of Caesar. God has shown his grace by sparing the lives of all those sailing with you."

I know we will make it to Rome eventually. But unfortunately, this ship won't. I told the crew that I had faith that God would spare them. But first we had to crash the ship onto an island.

Gotta go. It's almost midnight, and they're saying we might be getting close to land.

Day: Nope. Nothing

The ship wrecked. We got stuck on a sandbar, and the whole back was broken to pieces by the waves. But we all swam to shore. All 276 passengers survived. It was a miracle. We're on an island called Malta.

The people here have been very kind. It was raining and cold when we got here, but they helped us build a fire to get warm.

One sort of funny thing happened. Well, it's funny now. When I was getting sticks and putting them on the fire, a snake shot out and bit my hand. The people must have thought,

"First, a shipwreck, then killed by a poisonous snake! This guy must be a bad dude!"

But I just shook the snake off and nothing happened.

They were all looking at me, expecting me to die at any moment. But I'm writing this, so . . .

After the snake incident, they thought I must be pretty special. So when the chief official of Malta had a sick father, they asked me to help. I went to him, prayed for him, and put my hands on him. And God made him better. Then EVERYONE who was sick started to come to me. And God healed them too. Just think, that would have never happened if we hadn't shipwrecked!

I don't know how much longer we'll be here. The people are giving us supplies while we rebuild the ship. No matter what, though, I'm so glad God decided to take us on this course.

ME IN MALTA

That was some detour. If you had been on that ship and in that storm with Paul, you probably would have had a hard time understanding God's plan through it all. And yet, when we look back on it this many years later, it sure looks like God knew what was going to happen the whole time.

Maybe that's what it's like today too. You may go through hard times. Or the world may go through hard times. And while we live through it, we may not understand. But **you can TRUST that God has a plan.**

That's why a change of plans doesn't have to be a bummer. It could just mean that God has a better plan in mind.

Next time things don't go your way, ask God to help you trust in a bigger plan. Our God is amazing after all.

On Day TWENTY-ONE, you'll learn just a little about how amazing God can be.

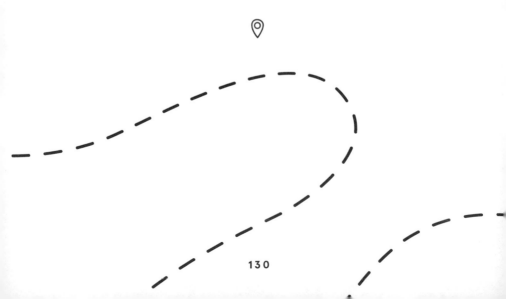

AN ANGEL HELPED PETER ESCAPE

ACTS 12:1-19

When you travel, it doesn't take long to discover how amazing God is. Like when you go to the beach and look out on the HUGE ocean God created. Do you ever wonder just how big the ocean is?

The ocean covers over 70% of the earth's surface, and over 94% of all life on earth lives in the ocean!

Or what about the mountains? Mountains are so majestic with their snowy caps and sky-scraping peaks.

The tallest mountain in the world is over 29,000 feet high, which is over ten times higher than the tallest building!

And if that wasn't amazing enough, try looking up on a dark night. The universe God made is so beautiful and even bigger than we know.

There are 200 billion trillion stars in the universe. That's 200,000,000,000,000,000,000,000 stars!!

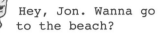

Hey, Jon. Wanna go to the beach?

Oh, no. Not after last time.

What do you mean?

I nearly froze solid!

You what?
At the beach?

Yeah! Remember this?

Just by looking at creation, we can know how powerful God is. And yet, sometimes we have a hard time believing. Even people who experienced God's power firsthand had a hard time believing.

Let's set the scene. Quick reminder: Jesus had died **and come back to life**! His followers were on a mission to tell the world about Him. But not everyone wanted to hear about Jesus. Some Jesus followers were killed. Some were thrown in prison. All of them were in danger.

Peter was in prison. A trial was scheduled, but it would not have been a very fair trial. Someone had to act quickly, or Peter's life probably would have been over.

The people who made up the early church prayed hard to God for Peter. Then the night before the trial, this happened:

 "Peter was sleeping between two soldiers. Two chains held him there. Lookouts stood guard at the entrance. Suddenly an angel of the Lord appeared. A light shone in the prison cell. The angel struck Peter on his side. Peter woke up. 'Quick!' the angel said, 'Get up!' The chains fell off Peter's wrists." Acts 12:6-7

That deserves a WOW! An angel appeared in a bright light in the middle of the prison, set Peter free, and no one noticed! Peter couldn't believe it. Literally!

"Peter followed him [the angel] out of the prison. But he had no idea that what the angel was doing was really happening. He thought he was seeing a vision. They passed the first and second guards. Then they came to the iron gate leading to the city. It opened for them by itself. They went through it. They walked the length of one street. Suddenly the angel left Peter."
Acts 12:9-10

Peter thought he was dreaming! God was doing something so amazing, even Peter himself was awestruck.

When the angel left, Peter finally came to his senses. He realized that God had sent an angel to rescue him from almost certain death. He went to the home of Mary (not Mary, Jesus' mother, but Mary, the mother of the guy who wrote the book of Mark). Many people had gathered there to pray for Peter. He knocked on the door.

"A servant named Rhoda came to answer the door. She recognized Peter's voice. She was so excited she ran back without opening the door. 'Peter is at the door!' she exclaimed.
"'You're out of your mind,' they said to her. But she kept telling them it was true. So they said, 'It must be his angel.'" Acts 12:13-15

Even the people who were asking God to save Peter couldn't believe that God would ACTUALLY save Peter! It wasn't until they opened the door and saw Peter with their own eyes that they finally believed.

That's how amazing and how powerful God is. God can do things that we can't even imagine. **You can TRUST that God can do anything.** So . . .

WHAT'S THE MOST AMAZING THING YOU'VE SEEN GOD DO?

In the space at the top of the next page, write something amazing you've seen God do. It could be making the sun come up every day. Or it could be something more personal.

The same God who made the oceans and mountains and the WHOLE UNIVERSE, also cares about you. You can go to God for any reason, with any thought or care. Talk about how amazing God is the next time you pray.

God's beautiful creation is a gift to people. On Day TWENTY-TWO, you'll learn more about God's greatest gift: Jesus.

DAY TWENTY-TWO

SALVATION IS GOD'S GIFT

EPHESIANS 2:8-9

The ultimate purpose of a journey is to get where you're going, right? But that doesn't mean you can't have fun along the way. There are a lot of different games that people play when they're on a road trip together. Road Trip Bingo, I Spy, the License Plate Game.

One game people play is The Alphabet Game. That's where you try to find a word on billboards and signs that begins with each letter of the alphabet. So let's play!

 On the next page, circle a word that begins with each letter of the alphabet. Once you've found a word that begins with a letter, scratch the letter off the letter list.

Letter List

A B C D E F G H I J K L M
N O P Q R S T U V W X Y Z

It's day twenty-two of our journey, so let's quickly summarize everything you've learned so far.

You understand that faith is trusting in what you can't see because of what you can see. And when you're on a journey of faith, you should never stop looking to Jesus. Moreover, the first step on a journey of faith is to BELIEVE in Jesus.

But knowing Jesus is only part of your journey. If you really want to be wise, you'll also DO what Jesus said. What Jesus said is very important. Here are some things Jesus said:

LOVE God. LOVE others. TRUST God. SHINE God's light. Tell the world.

Zowie! You've learned a lot. You're probably smart enough to play the xylophone!

Did you find all twenty-six letters? (Look at page 197 If you need to check your work.) If you found them all, you're a winner! Here's a trophy!

Congratulations! You earned it. It feels good to earn something, doesn't it? Not just when you're playing games but in life too.

When you study hard for a test, you can earn a good grade.

When you do your chores, you might earn an allowance.

When you prove that you're responsible in some way, you might earn new privileges.

But on your journey of faith, there's one thing you definitely can't earn. Check out what the apostle Paul wrote to a church in Ephesus.

 "God's grace has saved you because of your faith in Christ. Your salvation doesn't come from anything you do. It is God's gift. It is not based on anything you have done. No one can brag about earning it." Ephesians 2:8-9

"Your salvation doesn't come from anything you do."

Salvation may not be a word you hear every day. It just means you're saved from danger. In this case, salvation means you're saved from a future without God. Because of Jesus, your relationship with God is saved.

"No one can brag about earning it."

It doesn't matter how hard you study, how many chores you do, how responsible you've been, or how good you are at playing the xylophone, you cannot earn your salvation.

"God's grace has saved you because of your faith in Christ."

And that's good news! Because everyone really needs God's grace.

FUN FACT TIME WITH KELLEN

Kellen here! Here's a fun fact about me. I mess up A LOT. You probably do too. It is estimated that kids make an average of 3,000 choices every day. For grown-ups, it's more like 30,000. You're bound to choose wrong at least a few times. Every day. Here's a clip of me messing up a bunch:

Let's face it . . .

Sometimes people goof off when they should be studying. Sometimes people lie about the chores they've done. Sometimes people prove they're irresponsible.

You don't always DO what Jesus said. You may not always LOVE others. You don't always TRUST. You don't always SHINE.

But God's grace is really an amazing thing. Grace means that even when people have done something they know they shouldn't, not only are they forgiven, but they're also rewarded with a relationship with God that lasts forever!

Think of it this way: You break a rule, you get punished. We'll call that LAW.

Or this way: You break a rule, you don't get punished. That's what we call MERCY.

Then there's this: You break a rule, you don't get punished, AND you get taken out for ice cream! That's GRACE!

God's grace is way bigger than that. When Jesus died on the cross, He took the punishment for all the sins of the world. And then, of course, HE CAME BACK TO LIFE! **Jesus is a gift for everyone.**

When you pray, tell God how grateful you are for Jesus!

On Day TWENTY-THREE, you'll learn what you can do with the gift God has given you.

FAITH WITHOUT WORKS

JAMES 2:14-17

Gifts are great. It's fun to unwrap something new, sure. But more than that, a gift means someone who loves you was thinking about you when you weren't around. It feels pretty great to be cared about in that way.

Speaking of which, here's a question for you!

HAS ANYONE EVER BROUGHT YOU BACK A GIFT FROM A TRIP THEY TOOK?

On the next page, there's an empty space. Think about a gift someone brought you after returning from a trip or being away. Draw a picture of that gift in the display case, and write the name of the person who gave it to you.

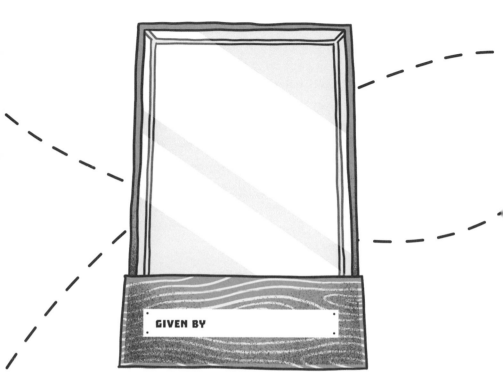

GIVEN BY

When it comes to gift giving, you may have heard the phrase, "It's the thought that counts." Maybe that's a little true, but the actual DOING counts more.

When someone GIVES you a gift, there's a lot of DOING involved, right? For example, they have to GO out to a store or MAKE something unique. More than likely, they WRAP the gift too. Then they have to actually DELIVER it to you. There's a lot of action and DOING involved in giving.

Well, a guy named James wrote something really interesting about the importance of DOING. Take a look:

"Suppose a person claims to have faith but doesn't act on their faith. My brothers and sisters, can this kind of faith save them? Suppose a brother or a sister has no clothes or food. Suppose one of you says to them, 'Go. I hope everything turns out fine for you. Keep warm. Eat well.' And suppose you do nothing about what they really need. Then what good have you done? It is the same with faith. If it doesn't cause us to do something, it's dead."
James 2:14–17

FUN FACT TIME WITH KELLEN

The book of James is found in the New Testament, and one of the craziest facts about that book is . . . James, the author? He was JESUS' OWN BROTHER!!! Bet you never thought about Jesus having siblings. But He did!! Pretty cool, right?

So, what was James talking about here? Isn't faith just BELIEVING? Doesn't salvation come from BELIEVING and having FAITH in Jesus?

Well, yes!

BUT . . .

Think about this: Say you went to school to become a surgeon, but after you graduated, you never ACTUALLY operated on anyone.

Or, what if you learned how to be an amazing carpenter, and you knew how to use every woodworking tool there was, but you never made anything. Ever.

That's basically what James was writing about.

Having faith is great. Believing in Jesus is really great!

BUT . . . when you have faith, you naturally want to do the things that come out of that faith. **When you believe in God's love, you SHARE God's love by what you do and how you live.** Your faith should make you want to treat people around you the same way Jesus treats you. Putting your faith into action is a HUGE deal. It shows the world Who you follow, but even better, it gives the rest of the world an amazing glimpse of a God Who loves them. Later, we'll learn more about how to make your faith grow. But first, on Day TWENTY-FOUR, another episode of *The So & So Road Show!*

DAY TWENTY-FOUR

THE SO & SO ROAD SHOW-EPISODE 4
(LUKE 12:15)

Once again, we join our friends Brandon, Jon, and Kellen as they adventure across the country.

Kellen is in the back seat staring out the window at a gas station while Brandon, who is driving again, does the same. Jon is not in the car.

They both look at their wrist watches at the same time and then look back at the gas station at the same time.

They've been waiting for a long time.

> KELLEN
> You think Jon's going to want to stop at EVERY gas station?

> BRANDON
> Yep. Every one.

Brandon sighs heavily and looks at his watch again.

> BRANDON
> I know that having patience is really important, but I gotta be honest . . .

147

I'm about to lose mine.

Suddenly, Jon comes bursting out of the gas station with a look of pure joy on his face. He's carrying a huge grocery bag filled with . . . something.

> JON
>
> GUYS! I GOT 'EM!

Jon gets back in the car and triumphantly holds up the grocery bag that is filled to the top with "Nutty Nougat 'Nanner Nom-Noms"

> JON
>
> I almost didn't get them all. When I walked in, they only had three. BUT, I asked if they had more stocked in the back . . . and guess what . . . THEY DID! I GOT' EM ALL!

> BRANDON
>
> That's great, Jon. Can we go now? We're already three hours behind.

> JON
>
> Oh, sure!! Let me just throw these with the others real quick . . .

Jon gets back out of the car.

There is a GIANT, HUMONGOUS bag sitting on top of the car that could easily be two stories tall.

*The little yellow car can barely hold
the weight of it.*

*Jon quickly climbs up the GIANT bag
and pours his tiny grocery bag
filled with "Nutty Nougat 'Nanner
Nom-Noms" into it.*

     JON
  That should do it. Nice and safe.
  What could possibly go wrong?

*It's becoming clear . . . that GIANT,
HUMONGOUS bag on top of the car is
also filled with "Nutty Nougat 'Nanner
Nom-Noms".*

*From the top of the bag, Jon triumphantly
yells . . .*

     JON
  WOO-HOO!

*Jon slides down the bag, gets back in
the car, and sits in the passenger seat
happily. Brandon and Kellen stare at him.*

     JON
  All right. The "Nutty Nougat 'Nanner
  Nom-Noms" are good and secure. ON TO
  THE NEXT GAS STATION.

     KELLEN
  Um, yeah, about that . . .
  Brandon and I would like to
  discuss something with you.

                    JON
Sure!

                  KELLEN
Have you noticed that you seem to be
obsessed with buying "Nutty Nougat
'Nanner Nom-Noms"?

                    JON
Me? What? No. You know me, I don't
like to spend money.

                  BRANDON
THEN WHY IS THERE A 20-FOOT-TALL BAG
FILLED WITH WITH NUTTY NOUGAT 'NANNER
NOM-NOMS ON TOP OF THE CAR?!!!

                    JON
Well, Brandon, it's simple. I LOVE
Nutty Nougat 'Nanner Nom-Nom bars.
And I can't get them where I live.

                  KELLEN
Understood, but do you need so
many of-

Jon's eyes start looking a little . . .
crazed.

                    JON
AND I need them ALL!

Bwaha.

BWAHAHA.

BWAAAAAAHAHAHAH!!!

KELLEN
Okay, then.

BRANDON
Jon? Listen to me very carefully.
You don't need all of these
candy bars.

JON
YES, I DO! I NEED THEM ALL!

BRANDON
But—

KELLEN
Jon. This has to stop. Take a look at
yourself in this handheld mirror I so
conveniently have.

JON
HUH—!? WHY—? BWAHAHA. BWA HA. HA—

*Jon sees his crazed face. He doesn't look
like himself.*

JON
HAAAAAAAAAA! What's wrong with me?

KELLEN
My friend, you have become totally
obsessed with Nutty Nougat 'Nanner
Nom-Noms.

BRANDON
And that's kind of the problem.

JON

But . . . how could buying as many
Nutty Nougat 'Nanner Nom-Noms as
possible be a problem?

KELLEN

Weeeeeelll—for one thing, our trip
was only supposed to take five days.
But, since you make us stop at every
gas station we see, it's taken 24.

BRANDON

AND, you're spending all of your
money on candy bars. Aren't there
better ways to use your money??

JON

Like, what kind of better ways?

BRANDON

I don't know, buy something you NEED
or . . . help someone else out?

KELLEN

Plus, when you get so consumed with
having more and more stuff, you often
forget to take time with friends and—
more importantly—God.

JON

Wow. You're right. I've spent so much
time getting these candy bars, I've
forgotten to hang out with you guys
or enjoy the scenery.

> KELLEN
>
> You know, Jesus actually warned us about this. Check out what Jesus said . . .

"[. . .]Watch out! Be on your guard against wanting to have more and more things. Life is not made up of how much a person has."
Luke 12:15

> JON
>
> Wow, that's a pretty powerful verse. I guess I was getting pretty obsessed with this stuff.

> KELLEN
>
> It can happen to any of us.

> BRANDON
>
> Um, guys?

> JON
>
> Thanks for pointing it out. I appreciate it.

> BRANDON
>
> Guys?

> JON
>
> So, what am I supposed to do with all those candy bars?

> BRANDON
>
> GUYS!?

                    KELLEN
      What is it, Brandon?

                    BRANDON
      I think I know what we are gonna
      do with your "Nutty Nougat 'Nanner
      Nom-Noms" . . .

*Brandon points to the windshield as Jon
and Kellen realize that the bag of "Nutty
Nougat 'Nanner Nom-Noms" has melted and
completely trapped them inside of their
car.*

                    BRANDON
      . . . we're gonna have to eat our way
      out of them.

                    JON
      That is a looooooooot of nougat.

THE LORD'S PRAYER

MATTHEW 6:5-13

Imagine for a minute that you're going on a trip away from your family. Where would you go? How long would you be away? Would you miss home? Whether you're a homebody or a great explorer—or a little of both—you'd probably want to have a way to keep in touch with the people back home, right?

Technology has made it very easy to stay connected to the people you care about. You can FaceTime, email, make phone calls, or send messages through social media.

Before technology, though, if you wanted to stay in touch with people while you were away, you could send a postcard. A postcard is a card with a picture on one side, usually of something you might have seen on your vacation, and space to write a message on the other side. So, on this imaginary trip . . .

REVEAL THE QUESTION

WHAT WOULD YOUR POSTCARD LOOK LIKE?

Design a postcard in the space below. On the front, draw a picture of any place you've been or any place you'd like to go. It could even be a place in your imagination! On the back, leave a message to someone you care about. Tell them what you've seen and what you miss about home.

Great! Next time you're on vacation, try sending a postcard. People get really excited when they get something in the mail!

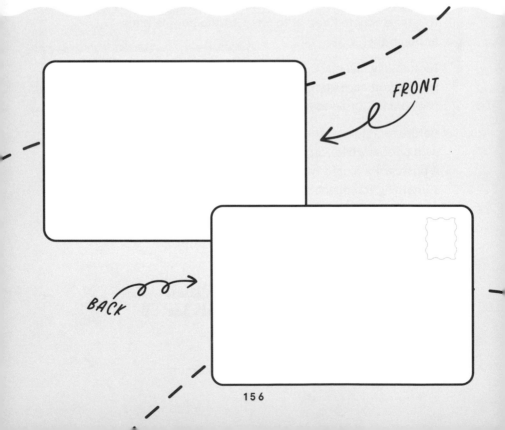

FRONT

BACK

FUN FACT TIME WITH KELLEN

Did you know over 250 billion letters are delivered every year? That's over 15 billion pounds of mail! That weighs more than the Great Pyramid in Egypt! Now I'm picturing a pyramid made out of mail. Whoa.

Hey, if you ever want to send mail to *The So & So Show*, you can. Ask a parent if it's okay and send us a letter, picture, or postcard to:

The So & So Show, 5870 Charlotte Lane Suite 300, Cumming, GA 30040

It would be fun to stay in touch!

Staying in touch with God is an important part of your journey of faith. You should make a habit of talking to God every day. If you don't know what to say, that's okay. Jesus gave His followers an example of how to pray. He said—

"This is how you should pray.
'Our Father in heaven,
may your name be honored.
May your kingdom come.
May what you want to happen be done
on earth as it is done in heaven.'"
Matthew 6:9-10

Quick note. Jesus wasn't saying you HAVE to pray these exact words. Jesus Himself prayed with different words all throughout the Bible. He just wanted to give you a template to pray in your own words. For example, instead of Jesus' words above, you might say:

"God, You are so awesome!" or "—amazing!" or "—incredible!"

What word would you use to honor God? _____!

Then, "God, what You want is better than what I want."

But Jesus' template didn't stop there. He went on:

"'Give us today our daily bread.'"
Matthew 6:11

You might say:

"Help me have what I need for the day."

What do you need? _____

"Thank You for all You've given me."

"'And forgive us our sins,
just as we also have forgiven those
who sin against us.
Keep us from sinning when we are tempted.
Save us from the evil one.'" Matthew 6:12-13

Forgive me when I do something I know I shouldn't or something that hurts You or other people."

"Forgive me for _____."

"Help me forgive people who've done something that hurt me. Help me to avoid situations where I'm tempted to do the wrong thing."

Talking to God can be that simple. You don't have to pray for hours. You don't have to get all the words right. What's important is that you stay in touch with God who loves you more than you can possibly imagine.

If you haven't already, say the prayer that you filled out above. Add more if you want. Tell God what you're thinking, what you're feeling, what your dreams are for the future. Anything! And remember—**talking to God can help your FAITH grow.**

And if you want to know something else that can help your FAITH grow, read Day TWENTY-SIX.

READING THE BIBLE

2 TIMOTHY 3:16-17

Technology is really amazing. Today, if you get lost while you're on a journey, you can use GPS to instantly find where you are and where you're going. It can even tell you how to avoid accidents and slow traffic.

It wasn't too long ago, though, that you could find yourself lost without GPS. In that case, you would need a map to help you find your way. Reading a map is a learned skill. So . . .

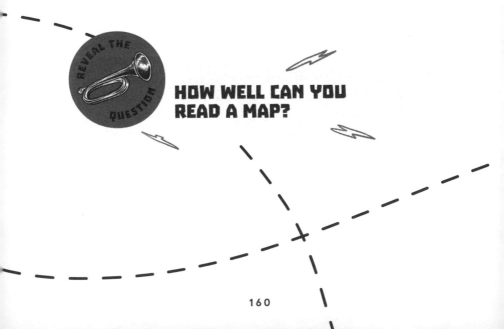

HOW WELL CAN YOU READ A MAP?

REVEAL THE QUESTION

Hey, Jon. I'm going out for a little while.

Okay. Don't be a stranger.

What do you mean by that?

You know. Stay in touch.

Stay in touch? You don't mean you want me to FaceZoom or ZoomFace or whatever it's called, do you? You know how I feel about technology!

I do. But the reader doesn't.

That's true.

Until now . . .

Help Jon and Brandon find the legendary golden cheese puff. It's buried somewhere on the map grid below. Use a pencil to map out the given directions. The compass star is there to help.

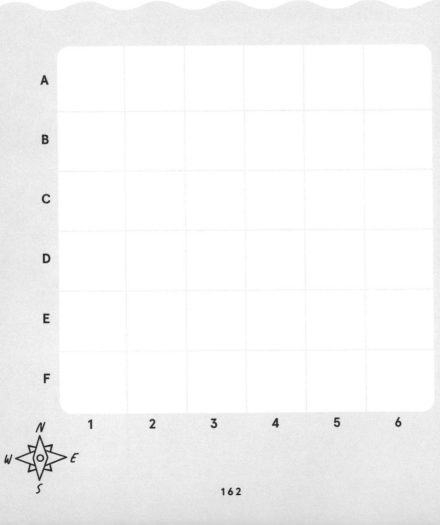

Quest for the Legendary Golden Cheese Puff

1. Jon and Brandon begin in box F1.

2. Travel two spaces east. (Hint: Don't count the box you started in).

3. Go one space north.

4. Mosey two spaces west.

5. Hike one space diagonally north east.

6. Climb two spaces north. (Hint: You should be in box B2. If you're not, you might want to start over. Hope you used a pencil).

7. Meander north east one space.

8. Jog three spaces south.

9. Ramble one space north east.

10. Stroll one space east.

11. Gallop one space south west.

12. Bustle two spaces east.

13. Skedaddle one space south west.

14. Dig for treasure. Draw an X on the spot.

**Check page 198 to see if you're in the right square.
If you are, enjoy the cheesy goodness of the legendary golden cheese puff!**

Maps are very helpful if you know how to read them. There's no actual map for your journey of faith, but the Bible comes really close. Check out what the apostle Paul wrote about the Bible:

"God has breathed life into all Scripture. It is useful for teaching us what is true. It is useful for correcting our mistakes. It is useful for making our lives whole again. It is useful for training us to do what is right. By using Scripture, the servant of God can be completely prepared to do every good thing." 2 Timothy 3:16–17

The Bible "is useful for teaching us what is true."

When you read the Bible, you can find out what's true about God, Jesus, the world, and you can even learn some truths about yourself.

The Bible "is useful for correcting our mistakes."

There is so much wisdom in the Bible. It's like a compass. Once you learn that wisdom, you'll know better what direction to go and what choices to make.

The Bible "is useful for making our lives whole again."

We know from the Bible that Jesus' death and resurrection made it possible for us to have a close relationship with God.

The Bible "is useful for training us to do what is right."

LOVE God. LOVE others. TRUST God. SHINE God's light. You learned all these things by reading the Bible!

Reading the Bible can help your FAITH grow. It's a good idea to make it a habit to read your Bible. If you're not sure where to start, ask someone you trust for advice. But don't feel like you have to read it all at once—or even that you have to start at the beginning! People read the Bible in many different ways.

When you pray, tell God how grateful you are that we have the Bible.

Hopefully, this journey is helping your faith get strong. After Day TWENTY-SEVEN, it could get even stronger.

THE CHURCH

HEBREWS 10:24-25

This has been a long journey so far, hasn't it? You're on Day TWENTY-SEVEN! Which begs the question—

WHAT'S THE LONGEST JOURNEY YOU'VE BEEN ON?

How many miles have you travelled at once?
_____ (If you don't know, ask or guess.)

How long did it take to get there?_____

How long were you away from home?_____

Long trips are fun—once you get where you're going. But sometimes getting there is a little annoying, especially if you're in a car with a bunch of people.

You know what makes journeys so difficult? Other people. People can be selfish and rude and loud and IRRITATING!

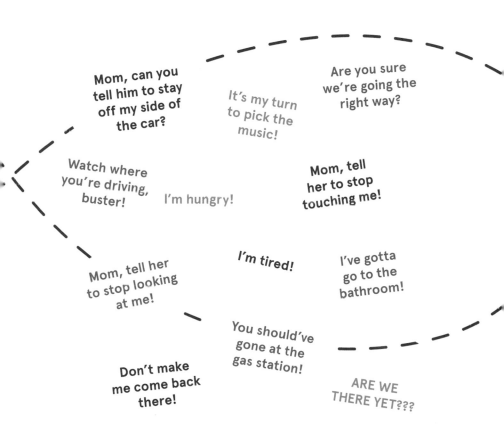

But . . .

Do you know what makes journeys so great? OTHER PEOPLE!

Other people help you experience things on your journey that you may have never thought of if you were alone. You may see sights you'd have never seen. Eaten food you'd have never tried. And when you're on a journey with other people, you'll have someone to talk to about it when the journey's over. It will always be an experience that you shared together.

You need people. Not just in your everyday life, but on your journey of faith too.

The writer of the book of Hebrews put it this way:

 "Let us consider how we can stir up one another to love. Let us help one another to do good works. And let us not give up meeting together. Some are in the habit of doing this. Instead, let us encourage one another with words of hope. Let us do this even more as you see Christ's return approaching." Hebrews 10:24-25

You've got to have other people with you on your journey of faith. That's why the Church is so important.

When you share your faith with other people, you can worship God together. You can talk about things in the Bible you don't understand. You can see how God is working in the lives of other people, and you can share how God is working in your life. You can "help one another to do good works" and "encourage one another with words of hope."

FUN FACT TIME WITH KELLEN

I'll bet you're wondering why the word "Church" is capitalized. Well, a church is usually a building where people go to worship God and learn more about the Bible. The capital "C" Church, however, is made up of every Jesus follower in the world. You don't have to be in a church to be with the Church. In fact, the early followers of Jesus met together in people's homes!

You can have faith in Jesus all by yourself. **But our FAITH is stronger together.** You need people in your life to help you on your journey.

Your journey, after all, isn't always going to be easy. Find out if it's worth it on Day TWENTY-EIGHT.

Jon, did you ever wonder what it would be like if we didn't do the show together?

You mean if I did the show by myself?

Yeah, or if I—

I wouldn't like that at all. I would be, like "Hi. I'm Jon." And then there'd be nobody to say, "And I'm Brandon."

No. Because I wouldn't be there.

"Hi. I'm Jon. And welcome to *The So Show*." It just doesn't work. Where's the "& So," Brandon? Where's the "& So?"

Good thing we're sticking together, I guess.

Don't scare me like that.

Sorry.

PAUL'S TRAVEL DIARY— WAS IT WORTH IT?

PHILIPPIANS

Let's start this day off with a promise from Jesus.

 "In this world you will have trouble."
John 16:33b

Um . . . promises are supposed to be a good thing. This sounds bad.

"'In this world you WILL have trouble'" (emphasis added).

Has that been true in your life? Have you had trouble? The apostle Paul certainly had his ups and downs. It makes you wonder if it was all worth it.

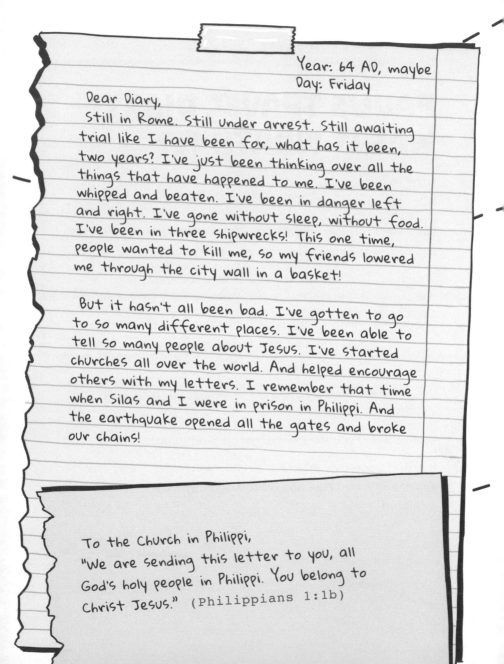

Year: 64 AD, maybe
Day: Friday

Dear Diary,

Still in Rome. Still under arrest. Still awaiting trial like I have been for, what has it been, two years? I've just been thinking over all the things that have happened to me. I've been whipped and beaten. I've been in danger left and right. I've gone without sleep, without food. I've been in three shipwrecks! This one time, people wanted to kill me, so my friends lowered me through the city wall in a basket!

But it hasn't all been bad. I've gotten to go to so many different places. I've been able to tell so many people about Jesus. I've started churches all over the world. And helped encourage others with my letters. I remember that time when Silas and I were in prison in Philippi. And the earthquake opened all the gates and broke our chains!

To the Church in Philippi,
"We are sending this letter to you, all God's holy people in Philippi. You belong to Christ Jesus." (Philippians 1:1b)

FUN FACT TIME WITH KELLEN

So, here's the truth. Paul never kept an actual diary . . . that we know of. The stuff in his travel diary in this book actually happened to Paul; he just didn't really write it down like this. What Paul did write were letters. Often, even while he was in prison, Paul wrote letters to encourage different churches around the world—some that he helped start. And those letters make up a lot of the New Testament! His letter to the church in Philippi is what we now call the book of Philippians. Some people think it was one of the last letters Paul wrote. Check it out sometime!

To the Church in Philippi,

"Brothers and sisters, here is what I want you to know. What has happened to me has actually helped to spread the good news. One thing has become clear. I am being held by chains because I am a witness for Christ. All the palace guards and everyone else knows it."

(Philippians 1:12–13)

Paul never stopped telling people about Jesus. He made sure even his jailers were aware of the good news.

To the Church in Philippi,
"I have learned the secret of being content no matter what happens. I am content whether I am well-fed or hungry. I am content whether I have more than enough or not enough. I can do all this by the power of Christ. He gives me strength."

(Philippians 4:12b-13)

Even in prison, Paul found a way to be content with what was happening. As he wrote, he had "learned the secret of being content." And the secret was Jesus. "He gives me strength," Paul wrote.

To the Church in Philippi,
"As far as keeping the law is concerned, I kept it perfectly. I thought things like that were really something great. But now I consider them to be nothing because of Christ. Even more, I consider everything to be nothing compared to knowing Christ Jesus my Lord. To know him is worth much more than anything else."

(Philippians 3:6b-8a)

And even though I don't know how my journey will end, I know that it has been worth it. I wrote this once, and I still believe it, "Our troubles are small. They last only a short time. But they are earning for us a glory that will last forever. It is greater than all our troubles."

(2 Corinthians 4:17)

Remember that promise we started off with today? It can be scary to think about, but Jesus' promise will come true. "In this world you WILL have trouble" (emphasis added). BUT there's more to the promise Jesus made:

 "'In this world you will have trouble. But be encouraged! I have won the battle over the world.'" John 16:33

When Jesus died, He paid for the sins of the world. And then . . . wait for it . . . HE CAME BACK TO LIFE!!! Jesus showed that death isn't the end of our journey.

Yes, you WILL have trouble. There will be ups and downs in your life, just like in Paul's life. Just like in everyone's life! **But FAITH in Jesus is worth it!** Putting your trust and faith in Him will help you navigate through the good times and the bad.

Our journey together has almost ended. Find out where we go from here on Day TWENTY-NINE.

HEAVEN

REVELATION 21:3-5A

"THE END IS NIGH!"

. . . well, at least . . . the end of this devotional. Which is kind of a bummer, right? It's been fun! BUT as the saying goes: "All good things must come to an end." Right?

How 'bout WRONG! But hold that thought and consider this first:

In this devotional, you've learned a lot. You've learned about Jesus dying and COMING BACK TO LIFE so we could be with God forever. You've learned about Paul's journey to tell everyone about Jesus. You've learned about Brandon's love of raw onions.

You've learned all the ways God wants to work through you to change the world around you. BUT . . .

That doesn't mean everything in your life is great. Let's face it, sometimes things can get pretty rough on this little blue planet placed in this big ol' universe of God's.

HOW CAN YOU FIX EVERYTHING THAT'S WRONG WITH THE WORLD?

Umm . . . wow.

That's a big question. Sorry, that's probably not one you can really answer or even accomplish. But here's the good news. This question is already answered by Someone else. (Did the capital "S" give a clue?)

John, one of Jesus' disciples, had a vision when he was older. A "Revelation," if you will. Here's what it said:

"I heard a loud voice from the throne. It said, 'Look! God now makes his home with the people. He will live with them. They will be his people. And God himself will be with them and be their God. He will wipe away every tear from their eyes. There will be no more death. And there will be no more sadness. There will be no more crying or pain. Things are no longer the way they used to be.' He who was sitting on the throne said, 'I am making everything new!'"
Revelation 21:3–5a

Oooh . . . ooooh . . . oooooohh . . .

Yes, Jon, I see that hand raised.

I know what these verses were about.

You do? Okay, then. Enlighten us.

Facial tissue.

. . . I'm sorry. Could you repeat that?

Facial tissue?

Facial. Tissue.

Uh-huh. 'Cause of all the crying stopping and stuff.

. . .

Because when you cry, sometimes you use facial tissue to wipe off the tears.

. . .

179

I mean, if you really think about it, maybe God will use facial tissues made of clouds-OOH-or angel wings!!

Jon?

Yeah?

Shhh.

K.

So . . .

This verse is describing one of the many things we can hope for when we follow Jesus. Jesus promises that at the very end of time as we know it, God will make "all things new." Another verse says God will create a new heaven and a new earth. And all tears will be wiped away from our eyes. There will be no more pain.

Basically, through Jesus, **you can have FAITH that God will make everything right in the end.**

Isn't that incredible? When we follow Jesus, we do it with the hope that one day, all the problems and struggles in this world will be made right. We keep our eyes on Jesus knowing that one day we will share an eternal home with Him.

But until that day comes, you are invited to help people see a little bit of what heaven will be like. Here's something to try:

 On the next page there are five STOP signs. Take some time to think of things that are happening in the world—unfair things—that don't line up with the loving God you've read about.

Maybe you heard about a storm or fire that caused a lot of damage. Maybe someone you love is sick. Maybe you have to try a lot harder to do something that seems to come easy for everyone else. Write one thing under each STOP sign.

Go ahead, turn the page and fill them in. Then come back here and keep reading!

Now, look at those things you just wrote. All of this will be STOPPED when Jesus makes things right.

Second, look at all of them again. Is there one that sticks out to you? Take some time this week to pray about it. Ask God to show you a way to help bring a little bit of heaven to someone who needs it in their life.

Then, talk with an adult you trust—maybe someone who has brought a little piece of heaven to your life—about how you think God is calling you to help others.

There's only one more day left in this devotional. You've done an amazing job getting this far. See you on Day THIRTY!

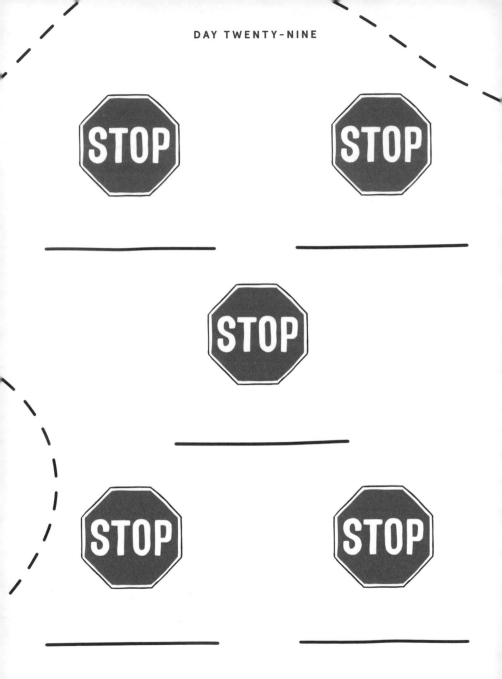

DAY THIRTY

THE SO & SO ROAD SHOW—EPISODE 5
(PROVERBS 3:5-6)

*Once again, we check in on Kellen, Jon,
and Brandon as their road trip comes to
a close.*

*Brandon, Kellen, and Jon are standing on
the side of the road next to their car.
They are looking up at something in AWE
as Kellen holds a giant map in both of
his hands.*

> BRANDON
> There's just no way . . .

> KELLEN
> I mean, the map says go straight.

> JON
> Yep. Straight ahead.

> KELLEN
> Well, this map maker has the job for
> a reason so, if it says go straight,
> I guess . . .

Suddenly, we see what they are looking at.

A road sign says:

LIFE MOUNTAIN
Straight Ahead
1 Mile (One Way)

And behind that sign . . . is an enormous mountain that's covered in winding roads, random tunnels, and snowy patches near the top.

> KELLEN
> . . . we go straight.

The guys get in the car and buckle up.

Kellen pulls out a cassette tape.

> KELLEN
> The map also came with a "HOW TO DRIVE LIFE MOUNTAIN" cassette tape we can listen to.

> JON
> A cassette tape? How old is this map?

> BRANDON
> Forget that! What's a cassette tape?

Kellen pops the cassette into the radio and a pleasant, soothing voice is heard.

> CASSETTE VOICE
> "Hello. Welcome to the audio tape 'How To Travel Life Mountain'. I am Solomon Oldes, your narrator. Shall we begin our journey?"

"Let's head towards Life Mountain.
As you move closer, the
first thing you'll notice on
Life Mountain is most of the
journey is 'uphill' . . ."

*The tiny yellow car starts to go up
a REALLY steep hill. — — — — —*

> SOLOMON OLDES
> "You may be nervous about driving
> up a steep hill."

> JON
> You had the brakes
> checked, right?

> KELLEN
> Trying to focus here, guys.

> SOLOMON OLDES
> "The steeper the hill, the larger
> the toll it can take on you and your
> car."

The car starts to make funny noises.

> BRANDON
> That doesn't sound good.

> KELLEN
> I can see the top of the hill! We're
> gonna MAKE IT! We're gonna make it!
> WE'RE GONNA . . .

*The car starts to struggle more and
slow down.*

> KELLEN
> . . . MAKE IT!?

The car stops working just before they get to the top of the hill.

> JON
> Guess we didn't make it.

> BRANDON
> WHAT ARE WE GONNA DO!? WE'RE STUCK ON
> A MOUNTAIN!

> SOLOMON OLDES
> "Difficulties will always arise on
> Life Mountain, but remember that
> overreacting and anger only worsen
> the situation."

> JON
> Yeah. Calm down back there. We can
> fix this if we work together.

(snaps his fingers.)

> I got it! We're in a movie script,
> right? Which means we have movie
> script strength! Let's see if we can
> push the car up the hill!!!

Jon and Brandon hop out of the car to try and push it while Kellen steers.

> SOLOMON OLDES
> "Road trips often remind us that
> journeys require the help of
> good friends."

> JON
>
> On the count of three! One! Two! . . .

> BRANDON
>
> WAIT . . . Kids, don't try this
> at home.

> JON
>
> Right . . . THREE!

> BRANDON
>
> MOVIE SCRIPT STREEEENGTH!

*And through the miracle of movie script
strength, they push the car to the top of
the hill!*

> SOLOMON OLDES
>
> "When victories on your journey
> arise, make sure to rejoice with
> those closest to you."

> KELLEN
>
> Woo-Hoo! We did it!

WOO-HOO!

MOMENTS LATER. *The little yellow car
travels towards a dark tunnel.*

> SOLOMON OLDES
>
> "There are times when traveling
> through Life Mountain that
> one may find themself in a
> dark place . . . "

> BRANDON
>
> Um, Kellen? Those head lights
> don't do much.

                    JON
I can only see a few feet ahead.

                SOLOMON OLDES
"If you do find yourself in a dark
place, remember to look for the
light. It may seem far away, but it's
always there."

                    JON
I think I see a light at the end of
the tunnel!

                  BRANDON
Head straight for it.

                  KELLEN
Focus on the light. Focus on
the light.

*EVENTUALLY, they come out the other side of
the tunnel.*

                SOLOMON OLDES
"There's no better feeling than
making it to the other side of a
tough situation."

                  KELLEN
WOOOOOOOOOOOO!

                    JON
WE MADE IT!   WOOOOOOO!

SOLOMON OLDES
"Along your journey you may encounter
obstacles that seem destined to keep
you from moving forward."

MOMENTS LATER. *The car sits next to a road
sign that says "Look for Falling Rock".*

*And there's a huge boulder in front of
the car.*

BRANDON
I think I see the rock they're
talking about . . .

SOLOMON OLDES
"You may also encounter unexpected
moments of incredible joy."

MORE MOMENTS LATER. *Instead of a boulder,
the car is now being blocked by a huge
herd of mountain goats. Of course, Jon is
already outside of the car hugging one.*

JON
I'M HUGGING A GOAT!

EVEN MORE MOMENTS LATER. *We see the car
slowly rolling to the very top of the
mountain and coming to a stop.*

Kellen, Brandon, and Jon get out of the car. Jon walks away to look at the view while Kellen and Brandon celebrate.

SOLOMON OLDES
"And always remember, even when you have reached what you think is your highest point . . ."

JON
Uh, guys? I think you need to see something.

Brandon and Kellen join Jon and look out into the distance. The three of them stand in awe as they see more beautiful mountains and hills and valleys.

SOLOMON OLDES
"There's always another experience, another surprise, another adventure waiting for you on the other side."

JON
Man, it goes on and on and on . . .

SOLOMON OLDES
"But do not get overwhelmed, traveler. Just remember what ol' Solomon says:

'Trust in the Lord with all your heart. Do not depend on your own understanding. In all your ways obey him. Then he will make your paths smooth and straight.'" Proverbs 3:5-6

KELLEN
Could not have said it better myself.

BRANDON
I'm just glad someone can keep
these roads and paths straight.

KELLEN
Well, fellas, with God as our guide,
even the most difficult paths are
easier to navigate. I say we keep
going on this journey.

BRANDON
I was thinking the same thing.

JON
Lots of ups and downs out there.

BRANDON
That's what makes it an adventure.

They get back in the car.

KELLEN
Everybody in and buckled up?

BRANDON
Ready when you are, Kellen!

JON
Yeah, what are we waiting for?, Let's
go . . . wait. What's that smell?

> BRANDON
> Oh. I've got some extra onions if
> anybody wants one.

> JON
> No thank you.

> KELLEN
> Windows down! Let's ROLL!

The car drives off as new adventures await.

The End . . . ?

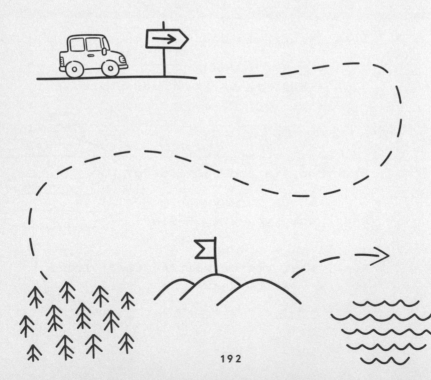

page 31

page 83

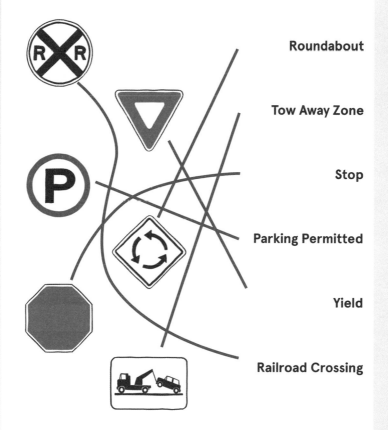

Roundabout

Tow Away Zone

Stop

Parking Permitted

Yield

Railroad Crossing

page 105

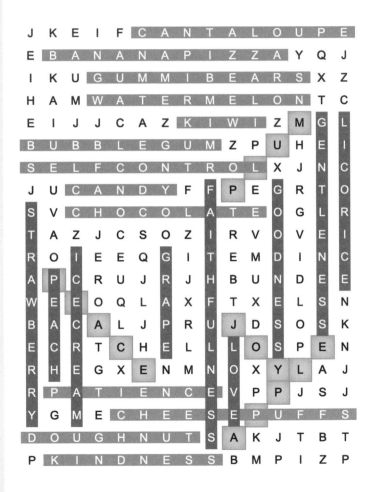

page 138

*I*t's day *T*wenty-two *O*f our *J*ourney, *S*o *L*et's *Q*uickly summarize *E*verything *Y*ou've learned so *F*ar.

You *U*nderstand that faith is trusting in *W*hat you *C*an't see *B*ecause of what you can see. *A*nd when you're on a journey of faith, you should *N*ever stop looking to Jesus. *M*oreover, the first step on a journey of faith is to BELIEVE in Jesus.

But *K*nowing Jesus is only *P*art of your journey. If you *R*eally want to be wise, you'll also *D*O what Jesus said. What Jesus said is *V*ery important. *H*ere are some things Jesus said:

LOVE *G*od. LOVE others. TRUST God. SHINE God's light. Tell the world.

*Z*owie! You've learned a lot. You're probably smart enough to play the *X*ylophone!

page 163

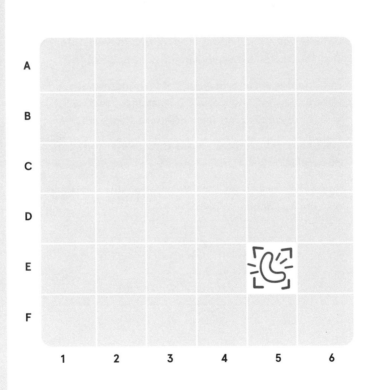

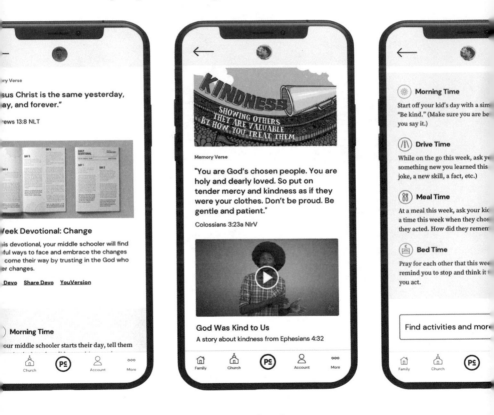